Faith Over Fear:
A Route 91 Story

X I MMXVII

By: Kelsey McKovich

Table of Contents:

Prologue

Everyone's story is different from that night and everyone is dealing with it differently. Some people saw friends and family members die, others barely saw or heard anything. Whatever we saw, felt, heard, or smelled it brought us all together and we are forever a family. I think it's truly incredible how so much hate brought much more love to this world.

I know we've all heard stories from people on the news, from friends and loved ones but I want to share my story and the aftermath of that event and how it shaped my life. You don't have to read this book in order; you don't even have to finish it. Read the chapters that stick out to you or read it in the flow that makes sense to you. All I ask is that you read "Chapter 1: X I MMXVII" first because that's the beginning of this whole process and metamorphosis of my life.

After tons of research and reaching out for help I came to the conclusion that there really isn't much out there for the average person struggling with PTSD after a shooting or traumatic event. I saw tons of resources for veterans or people who have been sexually assaulted or abused but I couldn't find any books for people who were thrown into a horrific event such as Route 91. So, I decided to write my experience that night and for the whole year after.

I am writing this book in hopes that it will touch someone out there that has been through something similar; so, they know they aren't alone. I hope there is at least one piece in this book that a person can relate to or at least ponder about and share. With the number of shootings out there in the world, especially in the USA, we need to stand together and get our voices heard to make change. We need to build support and let the world know we need to stand together not against each other.

As an educator, as a daughter, a friend, an author, and a victim/survivor, I hope this book touches you and helps you in whatever you're searching for in this world.

Chapter 1

X I MMXVII

At the beginning of 2017 I had made a decision that I wasn't going to let anything stop me from doing what I wanted to do with my life. I had a new drive and motivation to accomplish my goals. I had always been a very motivated individual and wouldn't let anything get in my way. I had lived with anxiety for a few years now and I wanted to change that. I created a "dream board" of all the things I wanted to accomplish and all the places I wanted to go in the world. On that list was lose weight, go to Europe, see the Grand Canyon, go to New York for a New York Giants football game, and attend Route 91 Harvest Festival in Las Vegas. Seeing my dream board goals every day was a constant reminder of why I was working so hard. It kept my positivity and drive moving forward instead of letting me dwell on the past.

When February approached and tickets for Route 91 went on sale, I immediately posted on Facebook that I wanted to attend, and I was either going to go by myself or with friends. I wasn't going to let anything stop me from accomplishing what was on my dream board. Two of my friends Jenna and Cierra messaged me and said they were down to go. I knew the three of us would have such a great time together. We all shared similar interests and even though they had never met, I knew we would all get along and it was going to be a fun filled weekend. It was the perfect plan because Cierra and I both bought our tickets to celebrate our birthdays, which were the week after Route 91.

Our tickets were purchased and so all we had to do for the next seven months was plan what we were going to wear, which hotel we were going to stay at, and what snacks and alcohol we planned on bringing. It was seven months of excitement and anticipation. I had gone to Stagecoach and country concerts before, but I was really looking forward to Route 91. Country music and Las Vegas all in the same weekend, it can't get much better than that!

During the weeks leading up to Route 91, we were finalizing everything, making sure we were all set for what we hoped was going to be the best weekend of our lives. Originally, we had booked a hotel down the strip from the venue but last minute, Cierra found a better deal at Tropicana which was right next door to the festival grounds, so it was a no-brainer to switch. That way we didn't have to walk far or worry about taxis.

Cierra drove up from Arizona and Jenna and I drove together from California. We met at the hotel Friday night and immediately freshened up and headed over to see Lee Brice and Eric Church. We stayed on the left side of the stage that night because we had arrived late and everywhere seemed too crowded to go explore.

Friday night was a great way to start our weekend. We bought drinks and rocked out to Eric Church. We weren't in the venue much that night, but we still had a great time and we were really looking forward to Day 2!

We were all excited for Saturday. I had my favorite outfit picked out. I had made a drink and laid out by the pool for a little bit. We had planned on entering the venue early to explore and see the festival in the daylight and pick our spots for watching the artists. At the festival we checked out different booths and listened to a performer at the Nashville Stage.

While at the Nashville Stage, I saw an older gentleman standing by himself with a walker. I felt bad that he was standing all alone, so I left my friends and walked over and started talking to him. He told me how a few years ago, when his second wife passed away from cancer, he decided he was going to travel the country and attend different country concerts. He had gone to Route 91 every year since they started. He had colorful festival wristbands wrapped around the base of his cowboy hat and he was looking forward to adding to his collection. He told me about his family and about all the states and concerts he had attended.

What I admired most about him was how he talked about how he didn't let anything stop him from what he wanted to do in life. He attends concerts and travels by himself all the time and it made me think more about my dream board and how this year I started making that change; and that I wasn't going to let anything stop me. This man had a huge impact on me that weekend and he probably doesn't even know it.

Thinking back on Saturday, I remember how happy the three of us were. It seemed as if nothing else mattered in the world. We just kept laughing and having a great time! Even leaving the concert we were still enjoying our time together by giving each other piggyback rides and just enjoying ourselves. It felt so wonderful to just let go and relax. We were excited for Sunday because we all love Jason Aldean, but we were also a little sad because we knew our amazing weekend would be coming to an end and we would have to go back to work and reality when the weekend was over.

On Sunday morning we went to "Top Golf" and had brunch. We had a few drinks at brunch and enjoyed our delicious breakfast. After eating, we made our way over to the venue where I bought cigars for my uncle (something my uncle and I have bonded over). We hung out at the Malibu Lounge and after some time walking around in the sun, we had become dehydrated and hot so, we decided to sit near a fan and stop drinking. We had been drinking all weekend and at this point we were tired of it (which was a life-saving decision and we didn't even know it).

Cierra and I sat inside at a bar in the venue and drank water and cooled off while Jenna went traveling throughout the grounds. When Cierra and I felt revived again, I wanted to try out the silent line dancing, which was up on the roof on the bar. It was fun to be above the grounds and see the festival from a different perspective and do some line dancing, which I truly enjoy.

After line dancing, we decided to see the venue from a much higher view and go on the spinning swing ride. We were a little nervous because it seemed like your typical sketchy carnival ride that could break at any minute, but we decided to risk it anyway. After riding the beast and surviving, we made our way back to the hotel room to relax before going back to hear the artists we were most excited about. I was happy because I didn't have to keep carrying my cigars around and we all had the opportunity to charge our phones and drink more water.

When we went back to the concert, we went to the right side of the stage and kept inching our way toward the front. We wanted to be as close as we could for Jason Aldean, since the previous nights, we stayed back and out of

9

the crowds. We wanted to push our way to the front so we could get a great view. We were able to get right next to the stage on the right-hand side (the Mandalay Bay Side). We were surrounded by some of the happiest people I have ever met! We were talking to everyone around us and the atmosphere was true bliss. A DJ came on before Aldean and he was playing lively, upbeat tunes ranging from top hits to songs from our high school days.

There was one woman who kept asking everyone where they were from and making connections with people. She would ask people their name and their hometown and if she heard someone was from the same area as another, she would introduce them. It was amazing how this woman just stepped out of the typical comfort zone of not talking to people you're surrounded by and was having strangers meet. We were all singing and laughing together; it was the calm before the storm. That woman had created connections that were much needed, without even knowing it. Who knew that because of that woman drawing us in and building relationships, it would contribute to our survival moments later?

When Jason Aldean came on, everyone cheered with excitement. We were ready for him to just rock out and put on the best show. I had seen him a couple of times before, but I had never been this close to him. I was ready to record every song to show my mom, who is also a huge Jason Aldean fan. We love going to Jason Aldean concerts together! I couldn't wait to show her all of our favorite songs being performed from such an up-close view.

Of course, he came out and started his show off right! He started his set with "They Don't' Know" and everyone was singing with him! If you've never been to a Jason Aldean concert, he basically makes the whole audience feel like a family. Everyone is singing together, and he brings such a passion of energy to the stage. He is one of my favorite performers to see live because you can just tell he loves every minute of being on stage.

His next few songs were just as energetic as his first and he continued to bring the heat, love, and enthusiasm to the stage as he always does. Unfortunately, we only got to see him perform six songs before he started to sing his last song, the last song some people would ever hear. "Some days it's tough just gettin' up, throwin' on these boots and makin' that climb…" These words will haunt some of us forever and to others, these words will forever have a powerful meaning to them. "When She Says Baby" was his "last" song that night. It was the song that would send shivers down my spine for months. It was the song that would instantly throw me into panic whenever it came on. It was the song that triggered flashbacks for me for months. It was the song that he started playing when the shooting began.

*Now, just for **warning** I will be describing in detail what happened to me that night. If that will be too difficult to read, you may skip to the next chapter. For me, this story and this part need to be shared. It is a healing process for me to tell my story and maybe it will be for you as well. Maybe hearing what happened to me that night, can help someone or open someone's eyes to the horror and terror of that night. Now it may be as difficult for you to read as it was for me to type. Please understand I am giving you a warning for a reason, it is horrific. I don't want this part to trigger flashbacks or anxiety for anyone, so if you feel any ounce of being uncomfortable please listen to your gut feeling and move ahead.*

As the song started, everyone was singing along and enjoying the atmosphere. Jenna was standing in front of Cierra and me. Cierra was on my left side (stage side) as I was closer to Mandalay Bay Resort. The first round of shots sounded as if someone lit fireworks off in the crowd to the right of us; it sounded ground level. It didn't sound like it was coming from above, but as if it was 15-20 feet away from us in the crowd. Even though it sounded like fireworks,

Cierra and I still ducked slightly and looked at each other with a look of concern. The sound was so loud, it had startled us and so our normal reaction was to lower our heads. I remember the look on her face, it was a look I had never seen on her face before and it frightened me. It was a look of fear and confusion.

In my mind I was thinking, *"Why are there fireworks going off at this time on a Sunday, Aldean just started his set there is no way fireworks would go off this soon."*

I could tell Cierra and I were still uneasy about the sound, but we slowly lifted our heads to the stage and the man behind us said, "Those were just fireworks, you're fine." Well, he was wrong.

Seconds later the second round started. The second round verified what we feared most. The second round is what haunts me the most; it was the round in which I was almost shot. As the round went off the gentleman standing right next to me, on my right-hand side, was shot in the arm. After he was shot, he turned and looked at me for help. All I could do was look him in the eyes and shake my head. I was helpless. I had never had someone look at me with a need of such help as that man did. His look of despair and pain still haunts me to this day. I will be out with friends and enjoying myself and all of sudden I see his face and that moment.

He looked at me for help. We made eye contact, and he said, "I've been shot". I couldn't mutter a single breath back to him.

After making that eye contact, I looked down at his arm where he was shot, and it was something I had never seen before. Just a hole in his arm filled with hot, red, blood, oozing out of it. It's his blood that stained my Route 91 wristband and my clothes and I couldn't help him. Even after being trained in first aid and holding a Red Cross certificate to help people in these situations, nothing prepared me for what I saw that night.

Luckily his friend behind him had pulled out a bandana or article of clothing and started wrapping up his wound. That's when I hit the deck and just crouched to the ground, trying to make myself as small as possible. The three of us, Jenna, Cierra, and I, huddled there and listened to shots continue and listened to the screams of pain from the people around us.

I knew I had to make contact with my mom and my boyfriend (at the time), Austen. They needed to know I was okay at that moment. I needed to let them know what was going on in case they didn't hear from me again. I wanted so badly to tell them I loved them but all I could manage to text was, "There is a shooter". I couldn't bear to type the words, "I love you", because I didn't want to believe that I could die at any moment. I knew if I typed those words it could mean the end.

They say the shooting started at 10:02 and I had sent those texts at 10:10. Which means we were down in the middle of chaos for eight minutes.

It's incredible the people whom you think about in the moments right before you die or might die. My mom and Austen were the ones I needed to tell most at that moment. I so very much wanted to tell everyone what was going on and that, so far, I was still alive, but I couldn't, because that's when we heard it again, another person next to us was shot.

At that moment, the woman in front of Jenna was shot. She was lying flat on her stomach with her partner next to her and she screamed in agony, "I've been shot, I've been shot in the butt."

She and her partner screamed out for help. We just sat there and stayed huddled after looking over at them. Once again, I was helpless. He tried to reach over and apply pressure to her injury as bullets continued to rain upon us. She continued to scream for help and so did everyone around us.

It was a complete war zone but for some reason I felt something like a shield, large arms, or wings covering over me, covering over the three of us. I had never felt that feeling before but for a second, I felt protected. I felt like there was something over me, blocking the bullets. Some say it was my dad, grandfather, and or God watching over us, sheltering us. As people right next to us were shot, their blood splattered on us, and we were unharmed. Jenna knew that wouldn't last. We needed to run.

After over 8 minutes of being right in the middle of complete chaos and destruction, Jenna looked at Cierra and me and said, "We're sitting ducks, we need to run."

She was right but it was like I had fallen into quick sand and I was stuck. My legs were stuck where I was; I was in too much shock to move. Cierra and I just sat there staring back at Jenna. We had heard what she said, and we knew we needed to run but couldn't do anything about it. Thanks to Jenna, literally pushing us to move, the three of us got up and ran for our lives.

When we started running, we became separated within seconds. We all took off in different directions; we didn't know where to run. We just knew bullets were literally raining from the sky above us, so where do you run, where do you hide? We needed a bulletproof umbrella to shield us from the metallic raindrops of death.

As I started running, another round struck. I hit the deck and was lying flat on my stomach with my head turned to the stage side where there were food and drink booths. As my head lay facing what once was a tempting food stand, I saw a woman sitting on top of what looked like her boyfriend/husband. He was covered in blood. His white shirt was dyed deep red now. She sat there pushing down on his wounds trying to stop the lava flow of blood erupting from his body. Her tears and cries for help as people kept running past were piercing to the ears. I turned my head away as I still lay there flat on the ground. I tried to make my body as flat as the earth I lay upon. I wanted so desperately to have the ground soak me up so I could escape this nightmare.

As my eyes scanned the ground I lay on, searching for answers, I saw another man flat on his back, not moving, covered in the same red liquid. No one helping him; just a man lifeless next to me. I lay there crying for a second realizing the two people that lay on the same ground within feet of me are most likely dead. If I continue to lie where I am, I am next. I didn't want to share the same fate as they did, so I stood up and continued running.

I decided to run towards the back of the venue, away from the stage. I knew running through the grass area would be a huge mistake because I would be tripping over lawn chairs and people's abandoned belongings. So, I veered right and decided to run through the main food and drink alleyway. I figured if the shooting continues at least I have places to duck and hide. I heard more shots and knew I had to take cover. My brain told me not to hide behind a bar because if there was a ground shooter, they could easily look over the bar and I would have no way of escaping; I would be an easy target. Just past the first bar stand I saw an ATM machine and decided to take cover there.

It's astonishing how the brain works when it hits "fight-or-flight mode". I knew in that moment that if a shooter approached me, I could at least have a chance of surviving because I could easily move around the ATM machine and have something to protect me in all directions. It was at that moment of hiding, where I looked up and saw police officers standing only feet away from me. I kept staring at them looking for guidance and support just as the people who were shot looked at me. I was looking up at my angels, the ones with the answers. They noticed me and motioned for me to run towards the back, past the second stage.

I got up and started running again. This time I knew I had to call my mom and grandmother and tell them I loved them. I couldn't believe I was still alive, and I just needed to hear their voice one last time and tell them I love them. As I was running, I tried calling my mom; no answer. So, I called my grandmother (at the time the three of us lived together and I knew my grandmother would be awake). She answered the phone and all I could say, in between breaths was, "Wake up my mom, tell her I love her. There is a shooter."

She could barely understand what I was trying to say as I continued running for my life.

I told her again, "Go wake up my mom, give her the phone, there is an active shooter, I love you."

As I continued running, I was getting closer to the second stage. I heard a man say, "Follow my son in the white shirt, he knows what to do. He is a firefighter." (I believe he said firefighter, but I could be mistaken). I could hear my grandmother, on the other end, walking up the stairs and waking up my mom. I never thought I would have to call my mom in such a panic and put that fear in her heart and in her mind. I told them I loved them and that I might die. I remember trying to explain what was happening, but I didn't even know what was truly happening. I told her," I am following a man because his father said he knew what to do."

As I uttered words and breathless mumbles on the phone, I ran past the second stage, through the back gates, and across Reno Ave to get to "The Tropicana Hotel" where our room was. I followed the crowd of people as we stampeded toward the hotel. There was a man kneeling at a backdoor entrance, holding it open for us. He was the," light at the end of the tunnel". He saved our lives, another angel lighting the path to safety.

We were inside a narrow hallway, running and pushing, to get further inside the hotel. People next to me were crying, some people covered in blood, others carrying injured loved ones or strangers. There was no way to determine if it was their blood or someone else's but it didn't matter. I continued to talk to my mom and grandmother as I hustled through the hallway with the others. At that moment I felt someone grab my shoulder and I almost screamed in horror.

I turned around and it was Jenna. I couldn't believe it was her! I cheered with excitement to my mom that I had found Jenna. For one second, I was ecstatic to see her until my stomach dropped and I noticed she wasn't with Cierra. I asked Jenna, "Where is Cierra?"

Jenna stated in the same breathless voice, "I don't know!"

We didn't know where she was but at least we had found each other. Once we were out of what felt like the longest hallway we had ever journeyed through, we had entered the casino floor and we turned right towards our hotel tower. We were going up to the next level and making our way down another long hallway when we heard people shouting, "They are shooting at the hotel; they are in the hotel." Then pandemonium struck again, and I was separated and alone, again.

People were charging toward our direction, it looked like a stampede. The thought flooded my mind that if I didn't get out of the way or run fast enough, I could get trampled. My brain went back into survival mode. I knew that if someone was shooting behind me, it was now open target practice for all of us in that area. So, I ducked behind a kiosk and told my mom and grandmother, "They are in the hotel shooting at us. I love you." I kept peeking through the shelves of glass, in between the merchandise in the stand, to look out for gunmen. When I saw it was clear I continued sprinting towards the elevators.

When I reached the cubby of elevators I ran towards a set of open doors before they could close. I tried squeezing myself in, but people pushed me out. So, I looked around and saw another open elevator. I ran over as the doors started closing on my hope of safety. I pried the doors open with my hands before they closed in my face. I was not going to let another glimpse of hope be shut on me, I was determined to make it. The people tried pushing me out and I stated sternly, "No, I am getting on this elevator I'm only on the third floor."

They allowed me to squeeze in with them when they realized I was not going to let anything stop me. As I stood facing out, I saw the doors closing on others. I felt sick to my stomach seeing the look of terror in their eyes and the doors closing on their helpless faces.

The doors opened on the second floor and no one budged. In panic, the 2nd floor button had been pushed and we all desperately wanted those doors to close and for the elevator to continue its path towards our safety.

When the elevator reached my floor, I peeked my head out to check and make sure it was safe before exiting. I quickly ran out and ran down the hall to my room. I had my key out and I fumbled frantically to get the key in the slot as my hand was trembling with fear and anxiety. Once I got it in and I shoved my way into the room, I closed the door as quickly as I could and started closing the blinds, turning off lights, and pacing the room. I told my mom, "Jenna and Cierra aren't here, I'm scared".

Moments later I heard knocking on the door. With hesitation, I looked through the peephole and saw Cierra and some other girl that wasn't Jenna. I opened the door and let them in. Cierra introduced me to Summer, a girl Cierra had found on her way back to the room. We all stood there shaking, when there was another knock at the door, and it was Jenna.

We had all made it back to the room and immediately checked each other to make sure we weren't shot. Our bodies were so numb from panic that we wouldn't have known if we were hurt or not. We all checked each other and saw that physically we were unharmed besides some scratches and bruises.

On the phone, I could hear the panic and confusion in my mother's voice. She couldn't find anything on the news about what was happening in Las Vegas, it was too fresh. We all were on the phone with loved ones but could only murmur whispers of fear and distraught thoughts. In our minds, we were surrounded by guns and thought we could be shot at any minute. It felt as if our world was darkened by black rifles, all aiming at us. After hearing people panic and run in the hallways of our own hotel, we had no idea what was actually happening beyond our locked hotel room door.

We could hear police sirens, helicopters, and the stomping of feet down the vulnerable hallways of our hotel. We wouldn't dare turn on a light, look out the window, or peek through the peephole on the door. We didn't want to know what was going on outside the "safety" of our room. We had seen enough. Every sound we heard, we jumped and then fell silent. In our minds, we thought the shooters could be outside our door and if they heard a single noise in our room, we would be exposed, and shot. Yes, I said shooters. We knew at that moment there was more than one shooter; there had to have been.

The four of us sat on the ground in between the two queen size beds. Jenna and I sat facing the window, with our backs up against the bed we had shared the last couple nights, while Cierra and our new friend Summer sat across from us against Cierra's bed facing the door. All we could do was sit there and try and talk to loved ones thinking this could be the last time we speak to them. We had no idea if more rounds would be coming our way or if there was a bomb planted at our hotel, or on the strip. There were so many unknowns that all we could do was whisper, cry, and pray. And that's what we did.

Just minutes later, our phones started blowing up. The world outside of Las Vegas was beginning to hear about the tragedy. I was getting calls and texts from so many people I couldn't even keep track of what was happening. I told my mom I loved her and said I needed to respond to others to let them know I am okay. I had gotten calls and texts from people I didn't even expect to hear from, especially so suddenly. I even had texts from numbers I didn't even have in my phone. I was feeling so many emotions at that moment, scared, loved, guilty, frightened, concerned, confused, and the list continues.

I had finally gotten a call from my boyfriend and I remember feeling an overwhelming feeling of relief hearing his voice. I wanted so desperately to tell him I loved him, but knew it was probably just the feeling of relief of being alive and having someone "by my side" that cared about me. We hadn't told each other we loved each other. Actually, we never got to that point in our relationship, but for some reason I wanted to say it that night whether it was true or not. I could hear the relief and desperation in his voice. He didn't know what to do or what to say. We both wanted to say so many things that night, but it was like the words were being stolen from us before they reached our tongues. He is a man of few words, but I wanted him to say more that night. Our phone call didn't last long but it was still refreshing to hear the voice of someone I cared about deeply.

After getting off the phone with him and staying in constant communication with friends and family via text and phone calls, it seemed as if that night would never end. I was so thankful we had our phones charged so we could contact friends and family and not have to worry about our phones dying on us.

When we felt it was safe to do so, we turned on the television to the local news station but turned the volume low enough so outside our doors it couldn't be heard, but just loud enough for us to hear the gruesome truth. We watched the man on the news speak of the tragedy we just lived through. Hearing the number of lost lives escalate was painful to our ears. We didn't want to watch or listen, but we needed to hear "what the hell had just happened" and what might happen next.

We were still so petrified, that when we used the restroom, we wouldn't even flush the toilet. We didn't want the sound of the toilet flushing to send a message to the terror outside our room that people were alive in our room. Our imaginations were traveling so far it was as if they teleported and traveled to different dimensions. We thought the worst of the worst. We thought all of Vegas was going to plummet into the "pits of hell".

We were getting texts about bomb threats at our hotel and the surrounding hotels. We kept hearing sirens and wished they would stop. Our minds wouldn't stop racing about what we had just seen and heard. Every noise sounded as if it was blaring from a loud speaker. Nothing felt silent. Every motion, every peep, every noise was magnified.

None of us slept that night. We couldn't. How could anyone sleep after experiencing the war zone that had taken over our beloved country concert? Jenna tried sleeping but the rest of us couldn't. Knowing I would have to drive home the second we were released from lock-down, I still couldn't close my eyes. I wanted so desperately to sleep and to wake up and realize it was just a nightmare, but I could barely sit on the bed. All I could think about was if I sit on this bed, a bullet will shoot through the window or wall and I'm dead.

The only place I felt somewhat safe was sitting in-between the two beds. They formed our bunker, our shield from the potential harm that could strike at any moment.

During that night we stayed in contact with people back home who couldn't sleep either. We continued to watch the news, wishing it wasn't real, and trying to wrap our brains around what was going on. We quietly packed our bags so that the second we could escape this twisted dimension of misery we were ready to leave. Then we just sat there, praying, crying, shaking, and being still.

We kept calling down to the front desk from our cell phones to see if we were released from lock down. We didn't dare pick up the hotel room phone because in our minds, if we even touched it, the shooters would see it was our room calling and come and shoot us down. Our imaginations ran to the deepest, darkest corners of the universe and beyond.

It wasn't until the wee hours of the morning that we got the glorious news we were able to leave. Summer left and went back to her hotel across the street. We made sure she kept in contact with us the whole way there until she was reunited with her friends. The second we knew she was safe we made our way down to retrieve our cars and escape this torturous world.

Leaving the room felt like we were leaving a part of our souls behind. It was that forgetting sensation you have before you leave for a big trip and you may have left your cell phone charger or wallet back on your nightstand. This time it was heavier, deeper than that. I wished that it was my charger I had left in that room, but it wasn't, it was my hope and security, trapped in that room. It was a part of us we couldn't get back and wouldn't get back. If this is what it feels like when your soul leaves your body, it's not a feeling I want to experience. It felt immortal and heavy.

Walking through the hotel lobby and hallways that we had just ran through, that we had just seen covered in blood and horror, was a feeling I wouldn't wish on my worst enemy. The air was a thick-coated layer of molasses. Walking, breathing, and just life itself felt as challenging as if someone was trying to stop us in our path. Just walking down, the halls and across the lobby, brought flashbacks and feelings of deep emotion. They were flooding over us like a tidal wave.

Dragging our feet down the haunted hallway I had just ran through fearing my life, I could see the window, the window that held the hole to hell in it. The hole that opened and released terror, and Mandalay Bay was its home. I could see it from where I had been hiding just hours before. It was the strangest and most disturbing feeling I had ever felt. We continued our lethargic walk to our cars without saying a word. We needed to process.

Jenna and I waited for the valet to pull my car around, while Cierra walked to hers. We made sure to drive past where she parked her car to know she got in safely. With the amount of mayhem that occurred the night before, we didn't know what to expect when we saw our cars. If people had taken cover there, run into cars fleeing for their life, or left blood-stained smears behind. It was reassuring to know our cars were just how we left them days before.

As we drove out of the parking lot, everything seemed to move slowly. Jenna and I wanted so desperately to look out the car's windows to gather information, to piece together what happened, but another part of us just wanted everything to turn off, to just focus on the road in front of us and go home.

We stopped for gas and snacks after leaving city center and then drove home. I was terrified to drive home. I hadn't slept in over 24 hours and I was still in shock. It was challenging to concentrate on the road. My eyelids felt so heavy, heavier than they had ever felt before. Yet I couldn't close my eyes. The second my eyes closed, I saw death, destruction, and anarchy. When I closed my eyes, I saw the man that was shot next to me.

The drive seemed to take days but within 4-5 hours we were back in Mission Viejo; we were back home. I dropped Jenna off at her boyfriend's house, where her car was parked. Then I made a stop by Del Taco because I hadn't eaten in over 12 hours. Food didn't sound good, but my stomach was growling ferociously. I needed to try and eat, especially something comforting.

I wanted to go home but didn't at the same time. I was scared to go home. Scared of what would happen next once I got home. Just being in the city itself didn't feel right and I was scared my house wouldn't feel right either. I even felt embarrassed. How could I go home after living through what I just lived through? I've felt embarrassed before, but this was a different kind of embarrassment, it was almost shameful. I felt guilty. How could I have taken a weekend off from work and responsibilities to go to Las Vegas to party with friends, and then put my family through what had just happened. I could have died for wanting to enjoy a weekend away. Even though no one expected that to happen, I still felt the guilt and I couldn't explain it.

I didn't want to go home, and I hated feeling that way. I took the longest way home to try and avoid it. For one of the few times in my life, I was scared to see my family. I didn't want to cry in front of them. I didn't want them to see me so battered and broken. I didn't want to feel the way I felt. The regret, the feeling ashamed, being scared, sad, worried, mad, distorted, guilty, and all of the above.

Pulling into the driveway of my house was difficult. Anticipating seeing my mother, my grandmother, and my two dogs was gut wrenching. I felt distant from them the second I saw them. It was like an outer-body experience. It was as if I was looking down at someone else hug my mom. I wanted so badly for that initial hug to feel like home, but it felt like there was a brick wall between us. I still didn't feel safe.

They helped carry my belongings in and the first thing I wanted was for my mom to cut my Route 91 bracelet off. It was stained with the blood from my concert neighbor who was shot just twelve hours prior. I couldn't stand for it to be on my wrist any longer. But it wasn't enough for my mother to cut it off and throw it into the trashcan. I wanted that trashcan to disappear. Just the thought of knowing that bracelet was in there was haunting.

I wanted it to be "trash day" just so that piece of evidence could vanish. I couldn't stand to even look at that trashcan. It reminded me that my bracelet was stained, tainted, and lost forever.

After disposing of the bracelet, I needed to shower; I needed to be alone. My mother helped take off my tainted clothes and started washing them for me, while I took some time to myself in the shower. I hadn't showered since Sunday morning and needed to wash away the dirt and clean my minor cuts. I needed to just sit there and feel the water wash over me, wash over my soul, or what was left of it.

Getting out of the shower and figuring out what to wear seemed more difficult then it needed to be. I wasn't sure what would feel comfortable and what to do next. I was so tired, yet still so jumpy. When my mom put my clothes in the dryer, the sound sent shivers down my spine. The rumbling and tumbling of the dryer sent me over the edge. I had almost experienced my first flashback. The tossing of the clothes and rattling of the machine sounded so similar to the way the bullets sounded and I almost hit the floor the second it started. I could feel my heart racing and the breath leaving my lungs, leaving me breathless and almost motionless again. My mom was there to comfort me and remind me that the thundering echo in the halls was just our dryer. I had never noticed the awful sound our dryer made until that day. It was so loud, so unnecessary.

The rest of that afternoon felt like a blur. I didn't want to see anyone. I didn't want to talk to anyone. I didn't even want to be there or be me. I just felt numb. People asked to come visit, but I turned them down. I didn't want that kind of attention. I just wanted to sit, process, and figure everything out. That night my boyfriend, Austen, did come over. The whole time leading up to seeing him I was so anxious and excited. I had replayed it over and over in my head of what was going to happen when I saw him. Would tears be shed? Would we share some crazy passionate kiss like in movies? Or would he just hold me and make me feel whole again?

When I did initially see him, it wasn't what I expected. I had imagined it being so much more and it wasn't. It was just like how I normally saw him, and I hated that. My hopeless romantic mind failed me on that one.

Of course, my best friend from elementary school, Brittany, came over bearing gifts and didn't listen to my plea of being left alone. The second she saw me tears were shed, hugs were given, and a glimmer of hope filled both our eyes. That was the feeling I was longing for that day and I am so glad she came and didn't listen to me.

That night, spending some time with Austen and Brittany was nice. I still didn't feel whole, but I smiled for the first time in almost 24 hours. I felt so weak and tired but was scared to go to sleep. I didn't want to sleep alone but I also didn't want to sleep in the same room with someone else. Would my tossing and turning disturb them? Would I have nightmares and wake up in panic? Or would I be so out of it that I wouldn't move from pure exhaustion? It ended up being a rough night, but I managed to get through that first night, the first night of the "new me".

Chapter 2

"New Normal" & "Survivor"

The whole next week after Route 91 felt strange to me. I took some time off work because I could barely sleep, and I just didn't feel like myself. How could I go back to work when I didn't even feel like me?

I remember, a few days after coming home, I was out driving around my city and seeing the flags at half-mast. It sent shivers down my spine. Seeing those flags lowered in respect to all of us that were there was gut wrenching. It made me sick to my stomach even though I knew it was to show respect and honor. Before Route 91, when I would see flags at half-mast, I thought it was incredible the way a city or company honored people from a tragedy, but now after living through one, I hated it. It just seemed like a reminder of what just happened. Having that hatred towards the flags, was just a horrible symptom of the new me.

On October 3rd, my mom and I put up Halloween decorations to help me forget about my nerves and anxiety. Halloween is my favorite holiday and decorating for Halloween is one of my favorite activities in the fall. That night we were set to have our annual "Ladies Halloween Night". The women in my family (aunt, cousins, grandmother, and my mom) make delicious Halloween themed food, treats, and specialty drinks, and we watch "Hocus Pocus" (my favorite movie). They were kind and offered to change our night to a different night knowing I had just returned from Route 91, but I thought it would be a distraction that was much needed.

I so desperately wanted to feel the incredible feelings of joy and happiness like I usually did on this night, but I couldn't. I felt as if I was watching someone in my place interact with my family. The food lost its taste, alcohol didn't even cause the slightest of buzzes, and I felt isolated in a room full of love and laughter.

When the movie came on, I had glanced down at my phone for a few minutes. I know every line to the movie and what the scenes look like paired with the dialogue. Nothing was new or going to shock me since I had seen this movie well over a hundred times.

Well, unfortunately, I was left shocked and startled. The sound of knocking on the witch's door sent me back to Vegas within seconds. I quickly left the room with the excuse of using the restroom, only hoping to not return. I went up the stairs, slid my body in between my bed and the wall and cried. The shots rang through my ears, the bodies dropped next to me, and the paralyzing fear was back but this time in my room.

I wanted everyone to leave. I wanted to be alone. I felt as if my favorite movie, my favorite holiday, and my family time were stripped away from me in my own house. I was robbed of the things that make me happy.

It seemed as if I had been up in my bunker for hours, but I knew it could have only been minutes. I tried to gather myself, as my mind slowly came to the conclusion that I was in my house and not on the festival grounds. I went to the bathroom to clean myself up and hide the streams of tears that stained my face.

As I came out of the bathroom my friend Chanel greeted me in the dark hallway. The only source of light was streaming through my bedroom entry. She hugged me and I cried. I cried for a couple minutes until my mom found us and then I cried to her. I wanted to disappear in that moment. I was extremely embarrassed. Their hugs and comfort were what I physically needed but not what my mind truly desired. I wanted to teleport to an island far away and just feel the cool ocean breeze on my face and to be alone.

My mom asked me if I wanted everyone to leave but I politely said, "No it's fine".

I slumped my way downstairs and joined everyone to finish the movie. I felt like I had to focus on every aspect, every sound, and every character in the film. I never had to concentrate so much on a movie before, but I was afraid that if I looked away for the briefest of moments, another noise would send me back into panic.

I hated that I couldn't just sit there and enjoy the movie like those who surrounded me in that room. I kept thinking to myself, "Is this my new normal, will I forever have to concentrate on everything all the time?" It was completely and utterly exhausting.

As the week progressed, I found myself watching every person's move. Focusing on their hands and their waist looking for signs of guns. I was on constant alert in fear that pandemonium would strike at any moment.

That same week, Austen and I went to Board and Brew for dinner. We sat outside on the patio because I felt that would be our "safest" option. I imagined being stuck inside the restaurant and someone opening fire. It would be treacherous to attempt an escape. But outside I could run and hide and have a greater chance of survival.

Of course, even that idea failed me. I was constantly looking at the tops of the buildings that surrounded us. My mind saw gunmen propped up awaiting their attack; I couldn't stop my eyes and mind from wandering. I wanted to enjoy a date night out with my boyfriend, but I couldn't.

While sitting outside, a car's headlights illuminated the wall in front of us and I lost it. It triggered a flashback and I needed to leave. The lights from the car reminded me of the stage lights when they had shown their spotlights upon us, while bullets fell from the sky.

After experiencing my first flashbacks and giving myself a break to heal, I decided maybe work would help distract me.

A couple weeks after Route 91 I was offered a long-term substitute teaching position to teach kindergarten at a public school in Yorba Linda. I accepted the position and successfully made it through my first week with the kids. I was worried I wasn't going to make it without worrying about an active shooter at our school site.

After my first week at the school, I got to see my cousin marry the love of his life that weekend. I was so excited to celebrate their love and party with my whole family. Moments before the ceremony started, we were all seated in our seats outside awaiting the arrival of the wedding party when a helicopter flew overhead. I felt my body duck and I went to cover my head in protection of what might rain down on us. My heart raced as if I had just run a marathon and I searched for answers. My boyfriend and mother sat in the row with me, but it was as if they weren't really there.

They held me and talked me through another flashback. I wanted to run. Run until I couldn't run anymore but I sat frozen in my seat trying to understand what was happening around me. My body was at the wedding, but my mind was in Las Vegas on October 1st, 2017.

I didn't want my mom to see me have a flashback, but she did. Everyone around me saw it happen. The sound of helicopters never bothered me until just a few weeks prior. It was extremely embarrassing to look around and see questioning eyes looking over at me while I looked back in fear.

Unfortunately, that wouldn't be the only flashback I had that night. When the dancing begun and we were all out on the dance floor, the song that still haunts me to this day came on.

For some reason the song "24 Karat Magic" from Bruno Mars continues to inhabit my mind and send me into instant flash back mode. I ran off the dance floor and hid around the corner. My mom and boyfriend helped adjust me back to normal but at that point I was done. Two flashbacks in one night is more than enough for anyone to handle.

The next day my friend Ben and I went away on a pre-planned trip to New York for a few days. I had moments of flashbacks there but nothing that inhibited my vacation.

After returning from New York, I continued working at the school until one Wednesday ruined my teaching experience for that academic year. It was right before lunch and I was trying to get the rowdy students to calm down so I could excuse them to eat.

There were a few troubled kids in that class who were challenging to manage. Those students started crawling under the tables and playing tag and weren't listening to the lunch supervisor or myself. Having to manage all of the students and see them running and hiding triggered a flashback. It reminded me of the people at Route 91 running and hiding for their lives.

I was extremely disappointed in myself, because for once in my life, I felt like I wasn't qualified for the position for which I was hired. I hated that. After the kids left the room, I hustled to my car with my lunch and called my mom, crying. I was absolutely terrified to set foot in that classroom again. I felt as if I had let the school, the kids, and their parents down. I was out of touch for moments and luckily the lunch supervisor was able to get the kids out in time for lunch.

I finished the day and left the school as soon as I could. I wrote a letter to the school thanking them and apologizing for the fact that I would not be able to hold up my end of our contract. The next day they called me into the office to discuss our next steps with my decision to leave the school. I was disappointed in myself, that I let them down, but I couldn't put my students' lives at risk in case a flashback happened again. I couldn't bear to have even more guilt on my plate.

I took a few more weeks off and came to the conclusion I wouldn't be able to teach full time in a classroom setting for the remainder of the year. It wouldn't be right. I needed time to heal and process.

In the middle of November, I found a position that I believed would be the perfect fit for me. It was a part time teaching position to work with one 4th grade student, one-on-one. Thankfully working with students one-on-one for this school year was the perfect situation for me, even though I missed the traditional classroom setting.

Feeling as if I couldn't do the job, I loved doing was hard. I wondered if I would ever be able to teach in a classroom setting again. I felt like this new version of myself might be useless and that all my hard work and professional degree would be flushed down the drain.

It was the night before Thanksgiving, I went out with my boyfriend and his friends to a bar in San Juan Capistrano. The same Bruno Mars song came on when we were all dancing and once again, I found myself running away. I ran and escaped in the nearby alley way and just cried. My boyfriend came to assist but it was no use. I was gone, once again.

For months after that night, this was my new normal. My mind searching for escape routes, imagining things that weren't there, and seeing those horrific moments from that night constantly flash in front of me.

I was beginning to believe that this was going to be my way of life forever. The terms "new normal" and "survivor" disgusted me. I didn't ask for a "new normal". I wanted myself back. I didn't want to be a new person, but it seemed like this would be it.

It seemed as though I died and came back to Earth as a completely different person, living a lie, pretending to be Kelsey McKovich. Kelsey McKovich had died that night and I was an imposter pretending to be her, I was living inside her body suit. I wanted to come back, but it was if a glass box of trapped emotion, fear, and anxiety kept me at arm's length. It kept me locked in and separated from those close to me. I could see my family and friends, I could hear them, I could talk to them but never touch them the way I had before.

Survivor was a word that was stained red for me. For years "Survivor" was just a show on CBS but now the word was a dark red hole of horror and pain. No one wants to be a survivor, but we all have to be, at least once in our lives. Some of us are survivors of cancer, of addiction, of losing loved ones, or of a mass shooting. It's incredible how within moments a word can change its meaning for you. I never thought that word would be tattooed on my soul forever.

I wear Route 91 shirts and sweatshirts that say "survivor" on them, but just to support my Route 91 family. I hate the term ''survivor" and didn't want to be a part of this new "club". But I believe wearing the shirts and sweatshirts acts as a bulletproof vest, and as a guide to those who were also there. I wear that merchandise, so they know I understand, and they are welcome to come hug me or say hello.

Throughout the year after Route 91, it was an uphill battle, struggling with the words "new normal" and "survivor". People want to change on their terms, not someone else's and unfortunately after that night, our lives changed, without us wanting it to happen.

I hated knowing this was my life now. I wanted to go back in time and change all of that but knew that it wasn't possible. No matter how many times people told me I had control over this, and I shouldn't let it change me, it did. As much as I tried to go back to who I was before October 1st, 2017, I just can't.

I know it's only been a year, and yes, I've made progress, but I can't even remember who I truly was before that night. I will never have that life back no matter how hard I try.

They say time heals all wounds, but does it? How much time will I need to let pass before too much time passes and I can't even remember who I was? I just have to accept the fact that I am who I am now and continue moving forward with my life. For some people, it may have been easy for them to get back into their routine and continue their lives, but for most of us it's impossible.

My biggest take away is, no matter how long it takes, it's okay to say this is who I am now. It's not easy and it still isn't for me, but that's life. You can't control everything life throws at you. The more you dwell on the fact that it's "hard" or "not fair", the harder you're making it on yourself.

Don't get me wrong, I still say "this isn't fair" or "I can't handle this" but I do find myself tolerating this life more now. Life isn't fair, that's a fact. If it was fair, then it would be heaven and not real life.

So, my advice for you is if you have a loved one that has lived through a life altering experience, just know they may not be whom you grew to know or grew to love. If you truly love them, you will stick by their side through every moment of doubt, every flashback, every nightmare, and every time they try to push you away.

If you have lived through something tragic, such as a mass shooting, and if you lose people in your life because they don't like your "new normal", or can't handle it, then you know they were never supposed to stay in your life. It's hard to imagine and hard to deal with but it's a blessing in disguise.

I lost friends and people in my life. It could have been because I changed, and they couldn't understand that or be there for me. It was hard at first, but looking back, I realized that it was meant to be that way. The people that stick through your new life are the ones you want to keep around. They are the true friends that can handle the good, the bad, and the ugly.

I even developed new and deeper friendships which I didn't think would be possible. The "friends" that I lost were replaced by these new friendships in my life now.

Things changed after that night, life is harder now and it will be for any survivor. If you have lived through something equally as tragic or even just traumatic in general, I pray that you find compassion and patience with this new life you will live.

Some people can't handle it and take their own lives. I would be lying if I said I didn't have those thoughts race through my mind from time to time. "It would be so much easier to not live anymore, to not face this new normal". But you have to push through. Giving up like that is giving into the evilness that already took so much from you. Don't let evil win. Don't let "new normal" represent the horribleness that has driven its way into your life. It did for me for a long time. It took a very long time and a lot of healing but it's possible to overcome those dark and scary thoughts.

This change is not easy. Just as a caterpillar changes into a butterfly, it takes time and patience. It only takes five to twenty-one days for butterflies to develop and it will take longer for you, but once you overcome your cocoon of fear, isolation, and darkness you will struggle feebly to fly, but you will successfully fly one day.

Your wings will make life beautiful for those you inspire and flutter past. Because you've lived through something so dark and lonely, you have the power to show what beauty can come from that. You can be the reason one person smiles that day by showing them your strength.

"New normal" and "survivor" are scary words for those it has impacted. Those words will continue to scar me, but they are just words. Over time the scars will fade away, not completely gone, but gone enough that you forget they were ever so prominent.

I prefer the words "warrior" and "strong" now. I refuse to let words victimize me as they once did. Just as "survivor" was changed for me once, I can change its definition once again.

Chapter 3
Flashbacks, Nightmares, Anxiety

In the following chapter I will attempt to describe my battle with the symptoms of PTSD. I will also convey some professional suggestions I have been given to help alleviate those symptoms.

Imagine you're sitting on the couch, watching the Super Bowl. You turn your eyes away from the screen at the exact moment a loud echoing sound emerges from the television screen. Within seconds you are seeing people dying next to you, you hear gunshots roaring past you, and you can smell the hot blood that is surrounding you.

You know you're still sitting in the living room, surrounded by friends but it's as if there is a screen placed in front of your eyes and you're watching a different show than everyone else.

You remove yourself from the couch and go outside and walk to your car to take cover. While walking to your car, your legs feel heavy and you're practically dragging your feet across the pavement. You look around trying to see what is truly there but all you see is darkness and terror. You know you're physically in a neighborhood surrounded by houses but all you see are people getting shot and hearing their cries for help.

Your hand trembles opening the car door and you climb inside and sink as low as you can. You cover your eyes and try and escape this horror that was placed in front of your face. It's like a mask that you can't remove, no matter how hard you try. You cry and shake, fearing these images will never stop but the fear and terror keeps escalating.

You feel your heart racing. It feels as though it will fly out of your chest from the amount of pressure. Your breathing quickens as if you're running for your life but you're not moving.

After several minutes of seeing those horrendous images placed in front of you, you come back to reality. You're exhausted, embarrassed, and want to be alone. Within seconds the flashback occurred, but it seemed to take a lifetime for it leave.

Then you have to face the harsh reality of walking back to the house and joining your friends. You have to sit on the exact same couch where the flashback started and filled with anxiety, you make your way back, with your head hanging low.

Unfortunately, that was one of my many flashbacks, months after Route 91. I was in the safety of a home filled with friends watching the Super Bowl.

For a long time, it seemed like my flashbacks would never end. I felt as if I was going to have to live in this alternate reality for the rest of my life.

I had such vivid flashbacks anytime there was a loud sound or when I would hear a motorcycle or loud engine. I had flashbacks when a bright light would flash, just like the stage lights at the concert. I had flashbacks during certain songs I would hear. I even had flashbacks with no trigger or warning. All of a sudden, I would just teleport back to Las Vegas and that horrific night.

Unfortunately, it's hard to control flashbacks. It takes time, practice, and some key tips from a therapist. Flashbacks happen whether you want them to or not.

One of my favorite things are fireworks. Seeing them on the 4th of July, at baseball games, or visiting Disneyland wasn't an option, it was number one on the agenda.

Well, after Route 91, I wanted them to disappear. They were one of my favorite things in the whole world and now I can't stand them to this day.

Going to baseball games, Disneyland, or celebrating any major holiday, now involves a checklist of escape routes and a week of restless sleep. These events come with an extra gift of flashbacks, nightmares, and anxiety that I didn't want or ask for. It's a party favor I wish I could return, but unfortunately, it's just the reality of the situation.

As much as I love going to baseball games and Disneyland, I have to prep myself in case of a flashback. Even now when I tell myself I am fine, get over it, "you've heard fireworks a handful of times now", I still get flashbacks. No matter how hard I try and deflect them, the vision of blood and death still flash in front of my eyes. It's like I am trapped inside a "Saw" movie but there isn't an end. I just have to live through this torture, as much as I try to stop it.

I've done things like take CBD oil, getting drunk, dancing, listening to music, or anything to distract myself during fireworks but the second the grand finale hits, I'm completely gone. I'm lost in the crowds of people running for their lives, screaming for help, and covering themselves from bullets.

Everyone says time will heal and it will get easier. I have noticed great changes in reaction time and "controlling" flashbacks, but I still have them and probably will for a while, or for life.

One of my most severe flashbacks was at an Angel's baseball game. It was the summer after Route 91, and I was there with a few of my friends. The stadium had a firework show and then played "The Sandlot" on the big screen. I thought, *what a perfect summer night.*

I knew the fireworks would send me into a flashback, but I went to the game prepared. I was ready to fight through it and watch the movie after. Unfortunately, the grand finale completely destroyed me. The sound of multiple fireworks popping at once and the echoing booming through the stadium sent me into a rabbit hole that spit me out in Las Vegas.

I sat their hugging my legs to my chest, shaking, crying, and plugging my ears thinking it would help. My friends Becca and Ben held me and kept trying to talk me out of it. They did everything they possibly could to save me from a flashback and I was so thankful they were there. After inching my way out of the flashback, I sat there with make up running down my face and shaken with anxiety. I made it through the first part of the movie that night but eventually just needed to be home.

Things that helped them, help me, was to find tangible things that weren't at the traumatizing event. I needed to stare or hold those things to help my body realize I wasn't there because this object or person was not there.

It takes a ton of practice and understanding but it helps. My dog Olive, certain people, and random objects have helped pull me out of flashbacks in the past.

If someone you know is having one, some helpful tips are: Say the date, the location, and list items that are

52

around that definitely weren't at the time of the traumatic event. Holding that person and reassuring them they are fine and there is no danger helps as well. Don't give up. It could take several minutes of resistance from that person, but they will be so thankful you held on and didn't stop trying. Just like I was thankful that Ben and Becca didn't stop and kept helping me that night.

When going through a flashback, you're in fight or flight mode with literally no signs of danger. Some people react by running, hiding, crying, shaking, or not even moving. Each flashback is different and unique, depending on the situation. So have patience.

I once went over a month without a flashback and then something completely random or something I thought I had control over triggered one and I was utterly defeated and depressed for days. I had gone so many hours and made it through so many situations without one and then I had one.

It feels as though you had completed this huge task at work, school, or in life and then someone tears it down and crushes your confidence and your hard work and you had no control over it. The walls around you crumble, the world goes dark, and you've lost.

I've had multiple times when I thought, "I've done it. I've made it past this, and I beat PTSD". Then, as if I've been hit by a semi-truck, that thought is shattered and broken. It's a horrible feeling, but I've overcome it with the help of my therapist, family and friends.

If you're a survivor, you will experience this a number of times. Every time it's hard but you have to keep pushing through. Don't let those negative and dark thoughts overcome you. It's easy to let that happen. Some of my darkest moments were the times after a flashback when I hadn't had one in a while.

At the moment, it's hard to see the progress, but in reality, it is progress. It's a huge step to go days, weeks, or months, without a flashback. When one comes rolling back into your life, it's easy to fall into that trap of despair. That's when you need people the most.

Most cases of people with PTSD who have committed suicide seem to be later in the healing process. It's because they've tried and tried to overcome this situation and can't seem to find the light at the end of the tunnel.

Just because it's been a couple months, a year, or a couple years, doesn't mean someone isn't still struggling. It's okay to still ask for help if you need it. Flashbacks are absolutely horrible, and I wouldn't wish them on my worst enemy. So, if you're a survivor, ask for help, even if it's the hundredth time.

If someone is tired of helping you or seems irritated, they may not be your person to go to anymore and I am sure there is someone else. People will get annoyed or bothered by it and that's okay. The BEST people are the ones that are patient and will always be there to support you.

If you're getting frustrated with someone who is still struggling with flashbacks, try and understand that they feel completely comfortable to be one-hundred percent vulnerable with you and trust you entirely. They are experiencing something out of their control. They didn't ask for this and don't want it to continue. Just hang in there and try to support them because they truly need you.

Nightmares are a completely different beast. Nightmares ruin sleep, make it difficult to concentrate the next day, and traumatize you where you never want to sleep again in fear of another one looming in.

In the beginning of my healing process, I saw so many Route 91 survivor posts about having nightmares and waking up in sweat from dreaming of that event. I didn't have that, and I felt out of the loop and wondered why I wasn't experiencing that as well. I was having flashbacks of the event on a regular basis, but my nightmares were more of people breaking into my house and holding me at gunpoint.

It was a weird feeling knowing people were having nightmares of the event and I wasn't.

In the last year and half, since Route 91, I may have had a few nightmares of the event but most of my nightmares have been about waking up to multiple guns drawn at me, with people dressed in black, staring at me, counting down to shoot. Then I wake up.

Usually I wake up catching my breath or dripping in sweat.

I never had an issue sleeping before Route 91. I always slept like a log and would have vivid dreams but never dreams that would be so horrific. Ever since Route 91, I struggle with sleep and nightmares. I've tried so many different things to help but it seems time will only heal this battle.

Some things that have helped are spraying lavender on my pillowcase, CBD oil, sleeping next to someone, taking sleep aids, and being so extremely tired from a long day.

Now these remedies have helped but haven't cured my nightmares or struggles with sleep. It's definitely been hard to imagine my life with consistent quality sleep ever again. Now I don't say that to ruin the spirits of survivors, but just know, that not all PTSD related issues will be easy. Sleep and nightmares have been one of my hardest battles yet.

When it comes to sleepovers with friends or boyfriends, it leads to this extreme sense of anxiety. What if I have a nightmare when someone is in the same room with me? Have I been tossing and turning and waking them up? Am I talking or mumbling my fears from the "reality" my brain is processing? Will it gross them out that I am drenched in sweat and I am a complete mess?

The fear of being judged when a friend or a new found love spends the night is hard. It keeps me from falling asleep as easily as the person in the same room as I am, unless I am just completely exhausted.

Even if I feel completely comfortable with this person, I still have that fear and anxiety of "what if I have a nightmare?". It's a hard habit to break especially with how frequently they occur.

It seemed like once my flashbacks lessened, the nightmares escalated. It is just battle after battle in this healing process and dealing with PTSD.

Everyone is different and may experience more nightmares than flashbacks, or vice versa or just a complete storm of both. So, I am not necessarily saying everyone will experience it the way I did, but you may experience one more than the other or at different times.

Your brain is consistently trying to process almost dying and that takes time. Some things may have been buried way down in the deep corners and caves of your brain, which you're only allowing it to process when your subconscious is awake in the darkness of night.

I've had so many nightmares that it got to a point that I became numb to the shootings that were happening in my dreams.

One dream in particular was that I was in a city that may have been San Francisco or one that was seemed similar to it. I was walking down a street when people started screaming and running past me and yelling that there was a shooter in the mall across the street. In that dream, I just looked in that direction and kept walking. I didn't bat an eye and it was horrible.

I woke up feeling like the worst person in the world. How could I feel nothing for the people suffering in my own dream? That dream haunted me for days because I couldn't stomach how I felt and how I reacted in that dream.

It also got to the point that I could wake up from a shooting nightmare and fall back to asleep and not be phased. It changed my whole mentality, feeling that if I am in that situation again, I will probably just die and that's my fate.

It was as though I had stopped letting the nightmares control my sleep, but they were completely changing who I was as a person. I hated how it was affecting me and my mental health.

It was almost as though after I came to that conclusion, that the nightmares only got worse and then started triggering night sweats and waking me up out of breath. It was as though my brain said, "No, you're not done with these thoughts, let's escalate them so you feel something again".

It's been a process ever since and things will continue to change in the future. It's just how you let it affect you. You can't let nightmares control your daily conscious thinking or you will go down a dark hole of things you never thought you would say or think.

With PTSD comes anxiety, it's like they are a two for one package. When you live through a traumatic event, especially in a situation where that shouldn't have happened, such as a concert or school, anxiety will follow.

You start to imagine that since a shooting happened there, it can happen anywhere. Your logical thought process is rewired and now it is filled with anxiety. The anxiety may be so bad that it starts making you paranoid or thinking irrationally.

There were so many situations after Route 91, where I thought another shooting will happen. My eyes became shifty and they were catching every sudden movement.

I had anxiety before almost any event, such as attending the movies, going to concerts, going back to work at a school, or pretty much any place with a great number of people. Sometimes even walking into a grocery store would be too much.

I would start watching every person's move, planning my escape route in case of a shooting, and fearing something horrible was about to happen. My heart would begin to race, I would feel light headed, and I couldn't concentrate.

These anxiety attacks and general anxiety came around out of the blue. "No knock on the door", it just came right in and started making a mess in my house and in my brain.

Anxiety planted thoughts in my head that weren't even rational. That the woman at the check stand next to mine at the grocery store would lose it because she forgot to get her husband's favorite ice cream or because she didn't have the exact change. Would she pull out a gun and start shooting? These irrational thoughts would spring up out of nowhere and happen anywhere.

It was as if anxiety was this little monster that just sat on my shoulder and would whisper terrible things into my ear. When I would shake it off and believe it was crazy, a soft whisper would answer back, "anything is possible, it could happen, but what if…"

I've had anxiety since before Route 91 but after, it got worse. It was always there, and it wouldn't go away.

Everywhere I went there could be a shooting. Then came the heavy breathing, the light-headedness, and the fear.

Some people asked about trying anti-anxiety medication, but I didn't want to medicate myself. I wanted to work through it and not cover my anxiety with a blanket for the rest of my life.

Talking with my therapist, family, and friends has helped greatly. Having them know, that I am struggling and may need a minute, helped lessen the anxiety. Some things that helped clear my anxiety were listening to music, writing about my fears, and working out.

When I've gone through a period of anxiety, having intense workouts has helped me take those emotions out in a physical way. Some of my best runs or best gym days have been when I just took all of the anxiety out of my head and into a physical situation.

Whatever you can do to release anxiety, find it and harness it. Try not to resort to drugs, alcohol, or other ways of life that could make it worse. Finding positive outlets to slowly diminish my anxiety has been a huge help.

I still have my days and nights filled with anxious thoughts. I still count and look for all the exits everywhere I go in case there is an emergency. I still plan my escape route and replay how to avoid being shot by an active shooter. But

I don't let it control me as much because I know there are ways, I can conquer it.

It's hard to say flashbacks, nightmares, and anxiety will ever go away because of what I went through and what many others have gone through, but I can say there are ways to help control it. Everyone is different and it may take several times or several different ways to find what works. Just know it's possible, you can get past it.

Chapter 4
Therapy and Resources

I started seeing a therapist my last semester at
Arizona State. I had completed my undergraduate in three
years and was getting ready to graduate in May. One
morning I was walking to my Clinical Psychology class,
which was my favorite because the professor was
dangerously good looking, and out of nowhere I felt like the
world was crashing down. I felt a slight sensation of tunnel
vision, and believed I was destined to die at that moment. I
immediately sat down on a bench breathing heavily. I
refused to ask for help or call 911 because I didn't want to
cause a panic and I feared the worst news, that something
was seriously wrong.

Instead, I sat there motionless trying to focus my
eyesight enough so that I could make it to a spot in the shade
and call my mom. I knew I wouldn't make it to class that
day and that caused my already heavy breathing to worsen.
When I made it to a shady spot, out of the line of sight of
others, I sat there for a while. I eventually made it back to
my car, drove home, and just cried in my bed.

I had had an anxiety attack before, but not one that
made me feel that amount of light-headedness or had given
me tunnel vision before. This episode gave me fear and

every time I walked to that class, I dreaded passing by the spot where I thought I was dying. It happened a few more times before I finally reached out to my friend's mom who is a Marriage and Family Therapist. I asked her what I should do, and she suggested I find a therapist in Arizona to help me overcome these anxiety attacks.

I had so much fear built up inside of me that I wouldn't be able to walk at my graduation. What if I had an anxiety attack there? Seeing a therapist helped, and talking to my friend's mom, Cindy helped as well. I was able to walk at my graduation, but I still had anxiety about it.

When my dad passed away, the following September, I had a growing pit of angst. A couple months after his passing, I started a new kind of therapy, that I was skeptical about at first. I was working at a chiropractic office where we offered massage and acupuncture. For those that know me, know I have a horrible fear of needles and friends and family were shocked when I said I was getting acupuncture treatments.

I received treatment for months and honestly, it completely changed my life. My intense anxiety attacks subsided completely, and I felt like a normal functioning adult, until Route 91.

I went back to the chiropractic office after Route 91 for some acupuncture treatments because I had seen such great results before with my previous anxiety. I cannot promise this enough. Acupuncture really does work. Acupuncture helps with anxiety and sleep. It truly is an amazing remedy. It helps rewire how your body functions and makes you feel incredible. But I couldn't just take care of my physical attributes, I needed to take care of my mental health as well.

The week after Route 91, I reached out to my friend's mom Cindy again for help. Without hesitation, she immediately started seeing me weekly. I truly believe seeing her weekly and addressing my worries, fears, and nightmares with her saved my life.

It was definitely hard at first and some weeks were harder than others, but I am beyond grateful I chose to talk with her, especially so soon after. I didn't want to talk to anyone else, I felt a sense of security and comfortability with her. I didn't open to her about everything and I know there will be things in this book that might surprise her, but it still felt good to let most things out.

Finding the right therapist to talk to after a traumatic event, will set free a lot of hidden monsters that were created due to whatever a person went through.

My first session with Cindy was emotional and difficult. I had known her since I was ten years old and she was there through all the chaos and craziness in my teen years spent with her daughter. But this was the first time I felt completely vulnerable and broken in front of her. She had seen me when we got busted for sneaking out in the summer of 2008. She had seen me through breakups that hindered my search for love. She had even seen me through the darkness of my father's death. But this time it was different.

When you go through a traumatic event like a shooting, you're stripped away of all securities, all your freedoms, and of your whole self. You don't come out of something like that the same person as you were before the event. It's almost like you have you BTE (Before Traumatic Event) and ATF (After Traumatic Event). Similar to how we tell things apart in history, such as AD and BC.

That first session, I felt as if she was having to get to know a completely new person. It was like my past was erased and I had to start over, from scratch.

I can't even count the number of times I told her "I don't want this 'new normal'. I want to go back to being me". She probably has that written on pages and pages of notes from our numerous sessions together.

It's healthy to talk to a therapist about your life, after a traumatic event. They don't judge you or tell you to move on or say you need to get back into your normal routines and life.

I trusted telling Cindy most thoughts, feelings, and things that were going on in my life. I knew I could unleash all the cringing details of my nightmares and flashbacks. If I told the people closest to me, like my family, they would either get tired of hearing it or be scared out of their mind and worry. I didn't need anyone to worry about me, I needed people to just sit there, listen to me vent and cry, and then tell me I am not crazy, because they have the knowledge to support what I was going through.

That's the hard thing for people to understand, that sometimes you don't want feedback, you just need to vent. I didn't want judging remarks, I didn't want someone else's thoughts or opinions, and I didn't want my family or friends freaking out, calling the nearest psych. ward in concerns of my wellbeing. I just wanted to be heard and have my thoughts validated.

There was so much I wanted to say to people but was scared to either say those things out loud or scared of how they would react. I just kept it bottled up, wrote it down, or told Cindy.

I told Cindy about all my nightmares and flashbacks. I hid some minor details about that night from her and some of the scariest thoughts I had ever had.

Not sharing everything is okay but if you're on the verge of completely and utterly destroying your life, I might suggest sharing that because I am sure friends and family don't want to see anything happen to you.

The first few months I had so much to say during every session. I was having weekly flashbacks or nightmares and had numerous moments of doubt that I could overcome PTSD. As time progressed, there were weeks that nothing new or life changing occurred, but I still saw her. I didn't want to break the habit of going until I was certain I could go on with my daily life without a crutch or aid.

I saw Cindy weekly the whole first year after Route 91. There were a few skipped weeks due to traveling or illness but for the most part I was very consistent. I think seeing a therapist weekly or biweekly for the first year is extremely beneficial and lifesaving.

A lot happens within the first year. You have to deal with talking with friends and family and addressing these changes with them. Sometimes they won't understand or say the wrong thing and it's good to talk to a therapist about it. You have to deal with work or becoming unemployed while you sort your life out. You have to go through the one-year anniversary of the tragedy.

Honestly, if it wasn't for my weekly therapy sessions that first year, I don't know where I would be right now. I am sure it saved my life. I had someone that I could vent to and unleash my dark thoughts. I knew what I said was going to be kept safe on the lines of the yellow note pad, tucked away in her office drawer. I didn't have to worry about bothering anyone with talking about another flashback or another nightmare. She never got tired of hearing my complaints, my worries, or my problems.

Trust me, I know it's difficult admitting you're going to therapy, but you don't have to admit it to anyone. It's no one's business what you need to do to take care of yourself and your wellbeing.

I constantly made up reasons about where I was going because I didn't want to admit how much therapy I needed. It took me a while before I felt comfortable admitting I was going to therapy weekly. I didn't want the world to know how broken I truly was and how much help I really needed. It can be embarrassing to admit the battles you're fighting and the disarray your mind is trying to sort through. What's not okay is finding inappropriate remedies to try and mask the truth.

There were nights I relied on alcohol, friends, or crying to try and cope with the dark looming clouds swirling in my head. Of course, those were only temporary fixes. Alcohol only numbed the pain for a night and then I woke up the next morning hung over, feeling worse than the night prior. Going to friends for help only left me feeling guilty, as if I burdened them and wasted their time, by sounding like a broken record over and over again. Crying helped at the time but then left my make-up running. When I caught a glimpse of myself in the mirror, it just made me feel defeated.

Talking to Cindy weekly helped me get everything out of my mind and made me feel validated. Talking to someone who had professional training helped me realize that what I was going through was normal. Hearing "it's normal" from someone without training or experience didn't help. They didn't know, how could they tell me what I am going through is normal when they literally didn't have any training or personal experience?

A month after Route 91, my church held a group counseling session one night. It was incredible to see how many people where there seeking help and reassurance that they weren't alone.

In the beginning, they asked everyone to stand who was a survivor of the shooting. Most of us stood up, showing that the remaining guests were family and friends, showing their support and wanting to learn more.

They did another exercise where they asked people to stand if they had experienced a flashback. They asked us to remaining standing or to stand if we experienced other symptoms they listed. Majority of us stood during the entire list of symptoms. This exercise really helped me feel reassured about what I was going through. The two friends who were with me at Route 91, were not experiencing everything I was experiencing, so it made me feel somewhat isolated. But to see the amount of people standing with me at that event helped.

That group therapy night really helped me realize that I wasn't alone, that there were others out there like me, experiencing the same burdens. I didn't go to any more group therapy sessions after that. I joined Route 91 Facebook groups and would sometimes vent on there. For a while, I would scroll through and read other posts from my new friends on the internet.

At times, scrolling through and reading those comments helped and other times it hurt. There are people on there that are kind and sweet and just looking for validation and support. Then, there are people that are rude and disrespectful. It's basically a giant melting pot of all kinds of people.

I made posts to the group where people were extremely hurtful, and it made me feel worse. There were posts I made to let people know they had helped and made me feel normal. They had made me feel as if wasn't alone anymore. I just had to focus on the good and ignore the bad. I would leave a disclaimer telling people I just wanted support and a safe space to vent. People would still ignore that and say some pretty hurtful words.

One post in particular was about seeing a man with a gun. It was the wee hours of the morning and I was driving to the gym. It was still dark from the night, so I was paying close attention to cars and for people. I saw a guy on a bicycle in front of me, making the same right turn I was toward the gym. As I got closer to him, I saw a black rifle strapped to his back and then I saw him turn and look at me and peddle faster.

I called 911 hoping they would listen to my plea for help and send a police car to patrol the area. He turned down one street toward the gym, and I made the second right turn down the same direction. After I turned, I saw him headed toward my direction, so I quickly made a U-turn in the middle of the road and stopped at the light, still on the phone with the dispatcher. He road right past my car and I was able to see every detail as he made his way down toward a local private school.

I had vented to the people on the Route 91 page how terrified I was, but I mainly got backlash. People saying, they have friends that ride motorcycles with guns on their back because they are going hunting or to a range. I was told that I shouldn't have called the police and that I over reacted.

It was heartbreaking to see people I trusted, tear me down like that.

My advice to survivors is that if there is an online support group, don't hesitate to give it a try. I actually met a couple of great people on there. It's nice knowing that I have friends with whom I share this weird bond. There will be thoughtless people on there, but you can't let them effect your healing process or what you're searching for. I had let some comments effect my process and I wish I hadn't.

If there isn't an online support group, create a support group in person or find one to join. Talking individually with my therapist is the route I chose but knowing others were experiencing similar things helped greatly.

Talking to a therapist and reaching out to other survivors helped me through this whole metamorphosis, but many other things helped as well.

After Route 91, it's rare for me to get a good night's sleep. When I do get some good sleep, it's basically a celebration, which is quite sad. I've tried "Sleepy Time Tea", taking CBD Oil, alcohol, and Advil PM's. Sometimes they help me get a solid night's sleep or even just for a few hours and then I wake up.

The nights I get the worst sleep are usually after another shooting or if I am sleeping in the house alone. I know from talking with other survivors, sleep is an issue for them as well, especially after another shooting.

There are many sleep aids and resources out there to help with these troubled nights but don't become addicted to sleeping pills or alcohol for help. It only makes matters worse and leads to drowsy mornings.

One thing that has really helped keep me sane and also helped a little with my sleep are my early morning work outs. On days I work out, and I mean really work out hard, I sleep better because my body is so exhausted from a hard workout and then working all day.

Once I was able to overcome most of my anxiety and fear, working out became something I did best, and all of the time. In high school I really got into fitness and weight lifting and I loved it. In college it became something I did to keep the weight off, or tried to, but it's been a part of my life since I was 15.

When I moved, the February after Route 91, I really made working out more of my daily routine. When I would feel frustrated or upset with this healing process, I would take my dog down to the beach and just run it out. Other times I would get a super tough work out in at the gym. Having these intense work-out sessions when my emotions were flustered, and fuming helped me overcome these uphill combats.

At the gym, by my new house, I met a group of incredible guys that I have become close to and they've helped me through some of these intense moments. They have taken time to train me, make me laugh on mornings I don't want to, and just helped make my workouts extremely enjoyable.

If you're someone who doesn't enjoy working out, I suggest finding a friend or group of friends that would make it fun. Honestly, it's really made a huge impact on my life and I am so grateful for this group of guys. They've helped make me stronger and encouraged me in times of doubt. Having a workout buddy or buddies can really help, in more ways than you expect.

The last remedy that has helped me through this whole process is writing everything out that I am feeling or experiencing. Most of my writing is what you're reading in this book. There are things I have written out that I would never share with anyone. I wrote things down on napkins, in the notes pad on my phone, typed it out, and even wrote things down in random notebooks I have.

Writing really helped me get what my brain was trying to process down on paper. This helped me try and figure out what my brain couldn't. It's as if things would get all twisted and bundled up. When I wrote things down it was as though I was untangling the yarn and stretching it all out, so it was no longer a tangled mess. I could really see what was inside the cluster.

Writing can help anyone, especially if you don't want to talk to someone about what you're going through. You can write everything down that you're feeling and then crumble it in a ball and light it on fire so no one would ever know. Just getting things out of your head and making your brain feel clear and free again, even if it's just a for day, can make a huge difference.

One thing I learned in a writing class I took was to just write, don't look back. If you just let your subconscious flow and you don't worry about spelling or grammar you can create a more perfect picture of your inner thoughts. Spelling and grammar will be a mess, but don't worry about that. Just write and let things flow out of you. You may learn something about yourself. It may help you understand what you're really feeling or experiencing and then you learn and grow from that. You can see what changes you need to make in order to move forward with your life.

It was hard to let go at first because seeing the little red squiggly line under misspelled words infuriated me to no end. I wanted so desperately to go back and fix it. After some practice and time, I would let it pass, and after finishing my thought, I would go back and make corrections.

Whatever you have to do to help yourself overcome these challenges, do it. As long as it keeps you on a healthy mindset and path to recovery, continue the battle. Don't fall victim to more destruction and pain. Take the steps you need to take to get your life back on track. Know you're not alone. There are a multitude of remedies out there. Some may work for you and some may not. Just keep trying and you will find what works for you.

Chapter 5

Family and Friends

Alright, family and friends of survivors of PTSD, this one's for you. If you're not a survivor of a mass shooting or a traumatic event, this chapter will probably be the most important to read. I will be explaining situations and experiences that have happened me personally and that impacted me after Route 91.

Friends and family will want to be there to support in any way they can. Sometimes it can come across as overwhelming or not enough to a survivor. It's honestly hard to tell how much attention is too much when we don't even know.

When I first came home and my mom and grandmother were right there to give me a long hug, I almost didn't want it. I didn't want that "special treatment". I just wanted things to feel normal. Of course, you want to completely embrace a loved one when they come home from a tragic event and I am glad they did but at the time it made me feel uncomfortable. Don't feel bad if your loved one feels that same way. We don't know what we're truly experiencing at that moment; we're still in shock for the most part.

If we don't cry or don't give you a passionate hug back, please don't take offense to that. We're in shock, mourning, and still feeling confused about what is real life and what just happened.

I had to try my hardest to seem comfortable or normal when I came home. It took an extreme amount of energy to not come across as extremely touchy and unhappy. It was completely exhausting. I wanted my family and friends to feel as if they could be natural and normal with me because I didn't want my life to change, even though it had.

At the beginning stages, it's encouraged to be respectful of personal space and if you're not sure, ask. Just ask that person how much space they want or don't want. I know for me, I desperately wanted the long hugs and the warm embraces, but when it happened or when I knew it was coming, I wanted to be isolated and left alone. It's a weird feeling and extremely uncomfortable.

We feel uncomfortable in our own skin. So, to feel someone else touching us, can make us feel worse. Now everyone is different but just don't take anything we do or say personally. We truly don't mean to offend or hurt anyone but when you're that uncomfortable and your mind and body is trying to process a million different emotions and stimuli, it's hard.

I am one of those people that was always happy for a hug or time spent with family and friends, but after Route, 91, I wasn't. I hated that feeling too, I felt like my personality had taken a 180-degree turn and I was someone else living in my body.

I remember feeling this way during my dad's funeral. I was so grateful for how many people had shown up, but I didn't want to talk to any of them. Survivors need time to process but they also want to know there are people there for them when we need them.

It's like we're standing on the side of a two-way mirror where we can see you, but we don't want you to see us. We don't want you to notice us or see us differently, but we want to see you and know you're there when we're ready to come out; when we're ready to show ourselves.

Here is a key that is extremely critical. We all heal at different times; don't try to rush us. We will do things when we are ready and trying to force us, won't help. It will only hurt.

There was one moment in particular that stands out to me and probably will continue to stick with me for years to come. It was the December after Route 91, about two months later. It was my friend's birthday and she wanted to go out to bars and clubs. I had tried going out to a bar the night before Thanksgiving a few weeks prior and it was horrible.

So, because of that, I knew that I wouldn't last long if I went out with her for her birthday. I was sick to my stomach thinking about all the "what if's". What if a certain song came on that triggered flashbacks? What if a shooter came in the bar? What if I couldn't get home safely? I fought this battle the days leading up to her birthday night. I didn't want to disappoint my best friend, but at what cost was it for me, to put myself through that anxiety?

I decided to leave it up to the night of and see how I felt. I figured she would understand if I just couldn't do it, and I would make it up to her some other way.

When the time came, I told her I just couldn't do it. I couldn't put myself through that fear and anxiety. I could tell she was upset but knew and understood. Another friend of ours didn't understand as well as the birthday girl did. That was hard, especially because she had been a best friend for years.

This friend had been through a similar situation and I expected her to understand more than anyone else. The night I couldn't go to the bars, she told me I "needed to get over it and move on with my life, that I shouldn't let this stop me from living my life". Hearing those words hurt me so deeply, like a knife that someone stabbed into my gut taking every last breath out of me. Someone I thought would understand, didn't, not the slightest bit.

I went home that night feeling like a failure. Feeling as if I could lose friendships over something I couldn't control. It wasn't fair at the time, but luckily, we still remain friends. We just don't really discuss this matter.

Survivors, there will be people who just don't think as much on an emotional level or semimetal level as you wish they would. That's just how it will be, there is nothing you can do about it, but don't let it ruin relationships. Just know there are still people out there who will give you the support you need. You can't listen to the people who won't "be there completely" for you. Some people just won't be able to understand.

Friends try to be a little more sensitive, even if you feel like you can't understand, ASK!

Ask us, "How can I help?" or say, "I want to understand, tell me what you want to tell me and how you need my help."

When you ask us questions about how to help or when you explain that you're trying to understand and want to understand, that speaks miles. At least show us you are trying to understand or trying to be there for us and think before you speak.

Sometimes what you think might not affect us, could. It could trigger us, even though before it may not have upset us. We all become a little more sensitive after living through a tragic event.

There was one day that I distinctly remember where a friend helped me drastically. One of my best friends, Emily, reached out to me with a text and said, "Kelsey I want to help, but I don't know how. How can I help you?" That text made me completely break down crying because it meant so much to me. I was impressed and shocked that one of my friends had found a way to help me when I didn't think there was a way to help.

That fact that she wasn't saying, "you'll be fine, you'll get over it, it will take time", but actually saw that this was going to take some serious healing and she had asked me how she could help, completely changed me. I was so incredibly thankful for that. Even though I still didn't know what I needed, just the fact that she knew to reach out like that helped.

So, if you're not sure how to help, tell your friend or family member, "I don't know how to help. Please tell me how can I help you? If you don't know right now, let me know when you're ready, and I will help in any way I can".

Now when it comes to flashbacks, that's a completely different story. You can't just ask us questions on what to do because we're not present. Mentally, we are not there with you. Our minds are back at that event. Flashbacks differ on levels based on the person and where they are in their grieving or processing of the event.

For me, I had such vivid flashbacks weekly, for months. Certain things would trigger them, whether it was auditory or visually. It's been over a year and I still get flashbacks. They were stronger in the beginning and I am in a little more in control over them now, but I still have them and will probably continue to have them.

All these tricks and tips helped me but please keep in mind that everyone is different and it's important to ask that person what he or she would like when one occurs. When the person you love is having a flashback, it's helpful to tell them the date, and what your surroundings are currently. Help them realize that it's not that moment in time; that they are in a different environment and different setting completely.

Explain and describe things that you can visually see that are different than what might have been there during the event. Pointing out more obscure or tangible things was extremely helpful for me. For example, describing people or animals that are currently near us that weren't at Route 91 helped.

Having dogs present helped pull me out of flashbacks because I never saw dogs in Vegas, especially that night. So, during a flashback if a dog was in our actual area, pointing them out really helped. It helped my mind come back and connect the two thoughts that I didn't see a dog so I couldn't possibly be back in Vegas.

For someone who has never experienced a flashback or know what one looks like, they come in all shapes and sizes essentially. There were flashbacks where I needed to go and hide and others where it looked as if I was just tuning out and not listening. Not all flashbacks will cause someone to run and hide. I have had plenty of flashbacks where people didn't even notice.

If that person you're with tells you they are having a flashback but aren't showing any dramatic changes or showing much of a reaction, still believe them and help them. Sometimes they won't even want to tell you. They might just excuse themselves for a minute and leave the area.

My closest friends who were with me through some of my flashbacks, figured out that I was having one when I would "check out" of our conversation for an extended period of time, or would excuse myself and be "missing" for some time.

At least for me and some people I've spoken to, after a flashback, a person might need an extra 5-10 minutes or sometimes longer to just gather their thoughts. The flashback itself takes a great amount of energy and can take a few moments to capture breath, gather thoughts, and just let the body rest.

It's not a one and done situation. After a flashback please be mindful of how much time someone will need afterwards to recoup. Also keep in mind how different each flashback is, that a person might not see or experience the same thing each time. Trying to understand them can be challenging. Something positive about flashbacks can be that sometimes you can track when they might occur and prepare for them.

My flashbacks usually occur with sounds that are similar to that of a gun. So, fireworks are a huge one for me, as are motorcycles or loud/repetitive noises. Certain songs that I heard that night also trigger flashbacks, as well as a bright light that is shown on me or in front of me.

For someone who lives through a mass shooting, any sounds that are loud or similar to that of a gun will most likely trigger a flashback. Even seeing a fire truck, ambulance, or police car with their sirens on, still gives me anxiety because we heard those sounds all night long.

There will be times when something completely random triggers a flashback. Our brains hold so much information that we might not even be able to trace how or why something triggered a flashback. It could have been something buried in our subconscious that we don't even have access to and won't be able to understand.

When it comes to flashbacks, I always wanted to be strong and fight through them. I didn't want too much help unless I was really struggling. The second I would break down, I wanted to be completely embraced and hugged and held. If you're near your friend while they're having a flashback talk them through it and let them know you're here for them.

I would sometimes get angry if someone tried too hard to help me during one. So, don't take offense if that person gets mad or angry. Their body is going through "fight or flight" mode without there being any sign of danger. It's exhausting and frustrating to experience. We don't mean the things we say or how we act during a flashback and the moments after one. If we do act out, we're usually extremely embarrassed by our actions and it can be hard to apologize.

Another thing that might upset a survivor is pushing remedies or therapy on them. I was lucky enough to know a therapist and feel comfortable enough to go start talking with her the week after Route 91. Not everyone wants to talk with someone, at least not right away.

I always spoke positively and comfortably about going to therapy to help cope with my PTSD. I didn't tell my therapist everything, just the things I wanted to talk about. I am sure she is reading this and realizing I didn't open up about a lot and that's okay. It is also okay to not talk with someone professionally, but find someone to talk to, such as other survivors or close friends.

I knew that if I didn't get everything out of my mind and talk to a professional, I might not be here today. I needed that escape and comfort in knowing the things I was going through were okay and normal.

I didn't feel comfortable talking to loved ones because I didn't want to burden them or scare them with these deep and disturbing thoughts and nightmares. I had friends from Route 91 that only felt comfortable talking to me or friends and family and wouldn't see a therapist.

So, try not to push what you think is right on them, everyone is different, and people need to find their own ways of coping. Now if someone is showing extreme signs, they might hurt themselves, step in but step in with an open heart and not aggressively.

There were definitely moments when my friends stepped in at the right times and saved me from a dark, destructive tunnel of despair and survivor's guilt. They never overstepped or pushed too much. It's because they asked, and I was open and honest with what I needed and wanted.

What someone shares with you might be hard to hear or they may not share everything, so ask, listen and be respectful. Don't immediately judge them or get concerned. We mainly just want someone to listen and be there. If we feel like you're ultimately going to judge or be concerned, we won't be as open to share.

So just communicate, check in, talk with us, be there for us when we need you, and don't forget that this doesn't just go away. We might live with symptoms forever. Just because it's been a month, a year, or several years, doesn't mean we're okay. Our lives changed forever that night and we will forever need support. So be there.

Chapter 6

6 Months Happiness Challenge

I started the 6 Months of Happiness Challenge on April 1st, 2018 because it would end exactly on the one-year anniversary of Route 91. I created an Instagram account especially for this challenge. I shared about it on Facebook on my personal page and on Route 91 group pages. I managed to get a few people to complete it with me. Whether people just followed or joined in, I was just making a conscious effort to make myself happy and spread happiness.

I would love to say that this was an original idea, but it wasn't. In high school, a close friend of mine was battling depression. This friend of mine was telling me about the "100 Happy Days Challenge" that she heard about from her therapist and asked me if I would do it with her. The challenge "rule" was that for every day for 100 days, you were to post on social media (any platform) something that made you happy that day. At the end of the 100 days you can see all the different things that make you happy in life.

I joined her in the challenge. Unfortunately, she was not successful in completing it, no matter how much support I gave her. I saw a huge difference in my attitude and really enjoyed it.

I did the "100 Happy Days Challenge" a second time and it really helped me focus on positive happy components in my life, compared to all the crazy twists and turns my life was currently going through. It was as if my life was stuck on "Mr. Toad's Wild Ride" at Disneyland. You expect it to be a fun kid's ride, but you enter into the pits of hell and you're not sure if you took LSD by accident or if the ride is really this out of sorts.

It took me almost 6 months after Route 91 to realize I needed to take some positive strides in my life to try and overcome this darkness of anxiety and guilt. I needed to see the reasons I survived. I knew 100 days would not be enough (no offense to the creators of the 100 Happy Days Challenge). I needed serious time and work.

So, on April 1st, 2018 I started my journey on the 6 Months of Happiness Challenge. I made an introduction post as to why I was doing it and welcomed others to join in.

My first official post was actually on Easter; which was great timing. How could someone be sad on Easter? My mom and grandmother had moved to Washington a couple months prior and I was so thrilled to be able see them for the first time since their move. My post included pictures of our Easter brunch and our wine tasting adventure. I filled the caption with a brief description of the images and hash tags such as "#route91", "6monthshappinesschallenge", and "day1".

My posts ranged from photos of dogs, food I cooked that I was damn proud of, minor steps toward my recovery, fitness accomplishments, and moments with friends and family. Some days were harder than others because I had some really hard days within those 6 months, but I made sure to post and stick to it.

Within the first two weeks of starting this challenge, my boyfriend of just over a year broke up with me. Luckily, I had already posted something that made me happy before my relationship crumbled within seconds. That morning, I ran on the beach with my dog Olive (which was something I was proud of since running was difficult after Route 91). The next day after our break up was extremely difficult, it was like part of my life was missing. Thankfully, it was a Wednesday and we had been consistent trivia night attenders at a local brewery every Wednesday night, so I had something happy to post about.

Another major Instagram post that I was so grateful to share about was my first night country line dancing since Route 91. It was Day 26 and I went with a fellow survivor that I had met six months prior, my friend, Victoria. We went to "The Ranch" in Anaheim, a place I had never gone before, but was excited to try out. I remembered some of my favorite line dances and even learned a couple new ones. It was a very challenging and emotional night, but I was so thankful that Victoria was there with me. After that night, I became a consistent line dancer again and it felt so good to be back doing something I loved.

At this point in my happy days challenge, I realized I was slowly getting my life back on track. I knew I wasn't completely there but at least I was making steps towards a happy and healthy life. I was working out regularly, I was going to more social events with friends, and I was starting to enjoy everything again.

On Day 58, I ran my first 10k race. It was crazy timing. Day 58 was a day I was running to prove to myself I could overcome a huge obstacle that was thrown in my path after October 1, 2017. I ran for those who couldn't, I wore my Route 91 tank top loud and proud. The second I crossed that finish line, I cried. I cried because I knew the 58 angels were there with me that morning, helping me overcome something I never thought I could. I also cried because my legs were killing me, and all I wanted to do was sit down after running for an hour.

That day meant a lot to me and it was so rewarding to be able to share that experience with the world (even though I had less than 200 followers). I was so blessed to be able to have Olive running by my side through the whole thing and to see my friend Becca at the finish line, waiting to give me a huge hug. Overcoming that day, got me excited to accomplish and share more.

Day 64 was another emotional and rewarding day. It was the day the Angel's baseball team held an event for Route 91 survivors. I had two of my closest friends there with me to support me, Becca and Emily. Even though Emily could care less about baseball, she still came to support my Route 91 family and that meant so much to me (more than she would ever know). We line danced under the "Big A", we cried, we laughed, and we soaked everything in. I was completely blown away that a team I have loved since I was a kid would take time to pay their respects to something that was my life now.

Thinking back to that day at Angel's Stadium still gives me goose bumps, it was truly something you can't put into words. It was a day I will never forget. I am so appreciative of those who were there with me and everything that happened that day.

Day 87 was also a huge day for me. After Route 91, I found it hard to work in a classroom setting or on a school site. I lived in fear of a school-shooting happening. With the increase of school shootings, I didn't think I could ever work in a classroom ever again. I thought my career and master's degree was flushed down the toilet. But on Day 87, I was offered a teaching position at a school that has a very unique set up. I would only teach two days a week and then my students were home schooled the other three days.

Of course, I cried. I couldn't believe such a school existed and was willing to take a chance on me. I had so many interviews at different schools and to a fault was too honest and told them my story. Due to my honesty, I wasn't offered positions because they feared I couldn't handle it. I almost started thinking about lying and hiding this part of my life just to get a job.

HCA came into my life at the perfect time. They took a chance on me and gave me my career back. On that day I was beyond thrilled that I was given a chance to teach in a classroom setting again. Knowing it was only two days a week was the perfect set up for me to ease back into teaching in a classroom again. It was a true blessing and I've met some incredible people at that school.

Day 97 was my first night dancing at Cowboy Country with my friend Jackie. She had told me about it a week prior and I was excited to try out a new country bar.

That night we met one of the DJ's on Go Country radio, David. First, I must say, what a gorgeous man. Secondly, because of all these challenges I was overcoming, I decided to take a huge chance. I got up the courage (thanks to Jackie) to just go up to him and ask for a dance. I had never met him before, but I had heard him on the radio more times than I could count and thought, "What's the worst that can happen. He says no?".

Well, we did share a dance together that night. I overcame another obstacle of just taking a chance and asking someone something I never would have done before. Every time we saw him at Cowboy Country, we shared a hello and hug and it felt like I added someone else to my Route 91 family.

Since that night, I have another family. When I go to Cowboy Country, I feel home again. Because I took this chance on going somewhere new and branching out of my comfort zone, I have a new family and a new home. I have experienced some incredible nights at C.C., and I will always love that bar.

Day 108 was the first day I started writing this book and created the table of contents for it. This day is the reason I am where I am right now (sitting in a Starbucks next to the San Juan Mission). Kidding! I am not still sitting there but I did get a decent amount of my writing done there and at other local coffee shops.

This day was special to me though because I finally made the decision to share what I had been wanting to do for months, truly share my story. It was July 16th when I made it public that I was writing *this* book. It was a really hard decision to come to because I was afraid of the criticism I would have to face. I knew deep in my heart that I needed to write this book and get this "stuff" out there. I wanted to share my story to help other people. The day I finally posted about it, I decided to take whatever came my way.

Day 119 was an accomplishment no matter how disgusting it was. I grew up the pickiest of picky eaters. I was so picky that when my parents took me to McDonalds, I would order a cheeseburger but take off the meat patty and fill the space in between the buns with French fries. People always asked me why not get a hamburger since you take off the patty anyways, well that's because bits of cheese would still linger on the buns and it was like my own little cheese fry burger. (Yah, I was a weird kid.)

On this day, for my brother's birthday, I actually tried new food. I have video footage to prove this. I tried chicken hearts and liver. It wasn't as bad as I thought it would be, but I don't plan on making it a part of my diet. Because of Route 91, and seeing my life almost come to an end, I was now trying things I never would have tried. I wasn't going to waste my life living in the comforts of the slow lane of life. I was now stepping up and doing new things. Needless to say, my brother was very proud of me!

With it being halfway through this 6-month journey, I was really branching out my comfort zone and realizing I was doing things I never would have done if it wasn't for Route 91. I really was living life as if there is no tomorrow, trying foods and saying yes to things I never did before that day.

On Day 121, I actually read the first draft of chapter 1 out loud to someone. It was terrifying because I wrote about things that I never said out loud. I wrote things that I didn't want to share but felt as if I should. I needed to include all the details in order to share my truth. Sharing these details for the first time was empowering. Hearing that it gave the listener goose bumps and chills was frightening because I didn't think I could have that impact on someone.

This day really made my book feel real. I started imagining what will happen when this really comes out, will it actually affect people who don't know me? Reading it to people I am close to, seemed like I was getting a biased reaction because we have a connection. It really helped my drive to write more because I wanted to share it with people who didn't know me.

Day 131 was my photo shoot day for Saddleback Church. I had decided to share my story with the whole church. They were going to put it on the back of all the pamphlets and on their website. Taking these pictures was so exciting because it was the first step to getting my story out there and being raw and open to strangers. Granted, I didn't write it but just knowing this was the first big stepping-stone to getting my story out there, to start helping people, was encouraging.

My first day of my writing class at Saddleback College was on Day 145. I had made a decision in the spring that I should take a writing class to really help steer me in the right direction, in order to write a book and get it published. I had no idea what I was doing, and I needed some guidance and support. This course was more work than I imagined but I grew so much from it. It encouraged me to read more and it gave me people to support my story.

I was one of the first people to share their manuscript because I had my first chapter done and ready for edits and reviews. I shared my manuscript and the whole class sat around in a circle of desks and each person shared their thoughts and opinions on it.

I was worried I wouldn't be able to handle the criticisms because this wasn't just any book, this was my life I was sharing with these strangers. I took every ounce of praise and critique and digested it the best I could. It felt so great to hear positive comments on my first chapter and not from people who actually knew me. It gave me hope that this book actually could make a difference one day.

Day 159 was my first day teaching 3rd grade at HCA. I was filled with emotions that day, mainly happy and excited ones, but still completely emotionally drained by the time evening fell. I was nervous about having a flashback or not being able to focus on teaching and constantly checking the doors and windows, but I made it through the day. I knew I was where I should be, and I was happy to be there and start this new journey.

The weekend after that, on Day 162, my story was shared all throughout Saddleback Church. My Aunt Doreen "stole" as many pamphlets as she could and pointed out to everyone that I was on the back cover and I was her niece. It was so great to have my aunt, two of my cousins, and a former student and her mom there that day. I had been reading the Saddleback Stories every week because hearing people's stories is inspirational and a true passion of mine.

I just couldn't believe that thousands of people were reading my story and seeing Olive and me on the back cover. At the end of the year, my story had become one of the top nine stories of the year at Saddleback Church. I had a handful of people reaching out to my family and myself about how they saw my story and couldn't believe I was on there. I honestly felt like a B-list celebrity for a day.

On Day 169, I met even more of my Route 91 family at a taping of "60 Minutes". Olive and I had been pulled aside to be privately interviewed but I was so nervous I couldn't get my thoughts straight and completely messed up every question they asked me. I didn't care though because I got to hear so many incredible stories from other survivors. I was overwhelmed with knowing we were going to be on TV. This was a very emotional topic, but I was so thankful I forced myself to go through this process. I met some incredible people that day.

September 23rd, 2018, Day 175, was one week before I returned to Las Vegas for the anniversary. On this day, some of my closest girlfriends joined me at the Jason Aldean, Luke Combs, and Lauren Aliana concert. This was my first country concert since Route 91. I was a freaking mess. I brought CBD oil with me to help keep me calm. I decided to be the designated driver because I knew if I wasn't, I would have drunk way too much alcohol due to anxiety and emotions.

This day meant so much to so many of us survivors. The last time we saw Jason Aldean, could have been our last night alive. So, attending this concert, which was held outside, brought every feeling you could ever imagine. We were excited to be there because we knew that after this night, we were going to get a part of our life back, a part that was stolen from us from some maniac hiding in a hotel room. We were going to finish what we started almost one year ago.

I finished the 6 months with a recap post of all the amazing adventures and experiences I had lived through. It was so amazing to go back through and really examine all of my accomplishments. I had done things I never thought I could do nor would want to do. Looking back, I was overcome with emotion because I was joyful, woeful, and proud all at the same time. I was happy because I did so much and completely transformed myself, I was sad because it took such trauma to bring such life into me, and proud because I set a huge goal for myself and I accomplished it.

Overall, I would highly suggest doing something like this if you're going through a dark time in your life whether it's depression or PTSD or you're just feeling down. I'm not going to say it's easy because there were definitely days that it wasn't easy. Some days it was like pulling teeth trying to find something that made me happy. Some days it was something simple like a home cooked meal or a new candle, or even just having time to sit down and write.

Each day doesn't have to be some grand event or major occurrence in your life. Just keep it simple and see what feels right to you. This challenge brought a new meaning of things to my life. I noticed more of the "small stuff" and I appreciated the little things so much more.

Research says that it takes 21 days for something to become a habit. So even if you just challenge yourself to be happy for 30 days, you will probably see a difference in your behavior and attitude. I am not promising anything, but it doesn't hurt to try it out and see if things change. Having a positive mindset was a huge factor in my healing and I am so grateful I completed 6 months of happy days.

Chapter 7

The Sticker

After Route 91, people started selling merchandise and stickers to raise money for the families of our fallen 58. Some people did it for their own profit, while others actually donated their time and worked on their products to support families. I immediately jumped on it and purchased some stickers and articles of clothing.

I enjoy wearing my sweatshirt when I travel because it's interesting to have interactions with people in other parts of the country that acknowledge Route 91 or were there or know someone who was there. It was such a major event in our history that it's shocking to me when I meet someone who has no idea what I am talking about or representing.

Some people feel that it's weird for us to wear sweatshirts or have stickers on our cars. They say we're, "glorifying or calling attention to a mass tragedy". In reality though, that's not true, we are wearing it in support of what we have gone through and supporting our Route 91 family. When people say we shouldn't wear the merchandise or call attention to that horrific day they don't see the background of it.

It's the same reason people wear cancer ribbons, to show support and love. That's why we wear Route 91 clothing or put stickers on our cars. We aren't trying to get negative attention and we aren't trying to continue reminding ourselves of the pain we went through. We are honoring those who were lost and injured. Seeing people wear merchandise or seeing car stickers in support of Route 91, makes the world feel smaller; it makes me feel like I am not alone.

In some of my darkest moments, I always seem to come across a Route 91 sticker or someone wearing a hat or shirt about Route 91.

There was one day when a man I encountered on the beach upset me, but on my drive home from that altercation, I saw a car with a sticker on it. The drive from the beach to my house is only 15 minutes, approximately 8 miles and I saw a sticker. Seeing that sticker on that day changed my mood around completely. When you have these representations present for the world to see, you don't know whom you can help or the difference it can make on someone's day.

On August 25th, 2018, I had a rough day. I kept notes in my phone and tried to write down moments of flashbacks, nightmares, or situations in my life that I feel was important in regard to this book. On my notes, I wrote about depression and how I just wanted to be alone, move to a new city, and just start over. The next day on the 26th, a car parked next to me with a Route 91 sticker on it. It helped me realize that if I move, I might not encounter these stickers or merchandise anymore.

Orange County and Southern California have a heavy population of our Route 91 family. It plays a major factor in how often I come across our symbol. If I moved, I might not come across it as much and it honestly has helped seeing them everywhere, especially when I need it most.

Probably one of the most significant encounters I had was on November 8th, 2018. It was the night after the shooting at Borderline Bar and Grill and I had cried all night long. I had to teach that day and there was no way to get a sub or get out of work. I needed to suck it up and push my emotions to the side.

I left early for work because I didn't want to talk to either of my roommates. I just wanted to get busy with work and forget everything from the night before. On my way, I saw a bus that was labeled 91. I had never seen or noticed this bus before on my way to work.

Seeing that 91 sent chills down my spine. It helped me remember that I have my Route 91 family with me, no matter what is going on in my life. It helped me get through the day, as silly as it sounds. Sometimes you just need a sign to help you go through something or realize something.

Since that morning, I have yet to see that same bus on my way to work. Whether or not you believe in signs, it's still nice to have these coincidences and encounters in your life.

Another pretty significant moment was the day we were leaving for the Route 91 reunion in Las Vegas. I had every emotion flooding through me like a giant tidal wave. I couldn't calm down or relax. I didn't know what to expect or how to act.

That morning I was driving to the bank to get some cash out for Vegas and I saw a car with a Route 91 sticker on it. I so desperately wanted to wave them down and give them the biggest hug. Seeing that sticker put a blanket of peace over my anxiety. It didn't last long but it helped for a little while and I was so thankful.

I've seen stickers on cars more times than I count, and I always see them when I need it most. When I need that constant reminder that there is a whole group of people out there that understand what I am going through.

I appreciate that there is a huge portion of us that live in Orange County. Since so many survivors are from this area, it is common for us to see each other on the road. It makes me feel sorrowful for those who came from different states or further distances to that concert. They probably don't see the car stickers as much as we do here in California.

I couldn't imagine living in an area where there wasn't a large quality of survivors. There have been so many times that I was grateful for running into a fellow survivor or seeing a car sticker.

With this thought circling my head from time to time, I usually travel with a Route 91 jacket or shirt. I wear my Route 91 clothing in hopes that it will spark a conversation, or it will help someone the way seeing those stickers helps me. Whether it's a survivor from Route 91 or another shooting, I wear my clothing to hopefully help send a reminder that person is not alone.

There was one situation where I was at Seattle-Tacoma International Airport waiting for my flight home after visiting my family and this man came up to Olive and me and asked about my jacket. He probably noticed Olive first, with her service dog vest on, and then read my jacket. It's kind of hard to miss since the words, "Route 91 Survivor" are in big lettering.

He asked if I was at the shooting and I responded that I was and then he proceeded to ask me more questions about my experience that night and thereafter. The way he asked these questions and the questions he asked didn't bother me. I was appreciative that someone wanted to know. He worded his questions so carefully and because he approached in such a gentle manner, I was more than happy to share my story with him. It's when people ask in a rude or harsh tone that it automatically builds a defensive wall around my feelings and responses.

So, if you're wondering if you should approach someone wearing clothing that supports something like a tragic event, just go up and be polite. Ask them if you can ask questions. If that person says no, then respect that and walk away. If a person says yes, then ask away. I am sure people are willing to share as long as there is respect and understanding.

Sometimes you don't even need to say anything. Every time I go to country bar, I usually see someone wearing a Route 91 hat or shirt. Just seeing them there, helps so much. Going to country bars or concerts still gives me so much anxiety. I get nervous that there will be another shooting. That's just how my brain has associated things now.

So, I have a Route 91 bandana on my cowboy boots. I keep it tied on there in case it helps someone else. When they see that bandana, my hopes are that it puts a sense of ease and calm over their stress or anxiety. I am forever grateful for the people that wear the merchandise and aren't afraid to wear it.

So, if you're not sure if you should represent a tragedy you may have lived through or know someone who has lived through it, I say do it. You honestly never know whom you might help. It could even help you, even though it brings up some uncomfortable feelings or emotions. If that's the case, you're being brave by putting it on.

I'll be honest. It was hard for me to wear the shirts and sweatshirts at first. I didn't want to be judged or looked at differently. It took a few months of wearing them to feel comfortable. I felt as if I had a giant sign that was so obvious to the world that I have PTSD because I was at a mass shooting. I soon learned that people are so focused on themselves, my shirts and sweatshirts rarely get noticed.

When they do get noticed, it's only been positive interactions. People asking questions or fellow survivors want to give me a hug or talk. Wearing gear has opened up so many opportunities to meet new people and even make friends.

I wore a Route 91 shirt when I went back to Las Vegas for the first time after that night. It was November 7th, 2017 and I had only told about 5 people I was going to do a one day turn around trip to Vegas. My friend Cierra and I were to meet about midday and retrace our steps. I didn't even tell my mom I that I was going, it was that much of a secret.

I had a 7am flight out of Long Beach and my friend Rachel drove me to the airport. I had missed my boarding time by 5 minutes and the ladies at the gate were not going to let me board, even though the plane still had its doors open and it wasn't even close to take off.

I was in complete hysterics, just a walking disaster and crying like a baby. They eventually let me board the flight, but I couldn't even find my seat because my eyes were pools of mascara and tears. This sweet young lady saw me crying and told me to sit down with her. The plane was practically empty, and I knew I was the last to board, so I sat down with her.

Besides the streams of tears rolling down my face and the fact I was headed to Vegas by myself, I believe my shirt helped indicate why I was going there. Victoria and I talked for a minute about how we were both at Route 91 and it made me feel so much better knowing there was someone on the plane who understood, and wasn't judging this poor girl, dragging her feet across the plane floor crying.

The flight attendant told me I had to go to my own seat, which was not necessary, because there were probably about 20 people on a plane that could seat over 100. It was still nice knowing Victoria was there with me. When we exited the plane, I waited for her and we exchanged numbers. We had lunch that day in Vegas and she has become one of my closest friends since.

On that day in Vegas, I got a tattoo in honor of that night. It is on my right rib cage and it reads 10.1.2017 in Roman numerals with "Psalms 91" below it. I got it on my right side in honor of the man that was shot next to me on my right-hand side. It's placed on my ribs because the ribs protect our organs and, on that night, I felt protection over me.

Many survivors have gotten Route 91 tattoos and I completely support it. My whole life, my family said I could never get a tattoo and that tattoos have a negative connotation. Well at 18 I got my first one, my grandpa's initials behind my left ear (above my heart for love and on my head for wisdom). Of course, my mom wasn't happy, but I had done it and that was that.

Since then, I now technically have 4 but they all have a special meaning. I think that's the important component when getting a tattoo. Seeing the beautiful Route 91 tribute tattoos show the creativeness that can come from utter destruction. Just like a tattoo is permanent on your skin, we have permanent scars since that night.

It's also nice to see people out in public showing their tattoos because it's just like wearing the clothing or having a sticker. It's a constant sign for people who were there or want to know more.

I have been questioned about people wearing Route 91 clothing, even though they weren't there. Now I can't speak for everyone, but I fully support it as long as they are wearing it in support of someone they love.

When my mom, Becca, Becca's mom, and I went to Las Vegas for the one-year reunion, we were given shirts at one of the events. I could see and tell they weren't completely comfortable wearing the shirts since they weren't at Route 91, and they were just here to support me.

I made sure to let them know that it's okay to wear it, you're supporting the people that were there and if someone questions them or says something in regard to them wearing the shirt that they could just explain. I loved that we all wore our shirts on the morning of October 1st, 2018. It showed how much these ladies love and care about me.

So, if you're unsure if you should represent a tragic event by wearing merchandise or putting a sticker on your car, I say do it if it makes you happy. If it helps you cope and it doesn't bring turmoil into your life, do it. You never know how it might help someone or brighten their day knowing they aren't alone.

Chapter 8
You Don't Look Blind

I got my dog Olive when she was just eight weeks old. After my father passed away unexpectedly in September 2014, my mom thought it would be a great idea to get me a dog for Christmas. We had talked about getting another dog as a family but when my dad passed it was a given, we needed new life in our home.

When talking with dog adoption agencies it was suggested that since our new fluffy addition would be for me, I should pick out the dog. So instead of surprising me Christmas morning, my mom told me on a random week day that she had been looking at dogs but that it should be my decision. I was thrilled; I couldn't wait to find my new companion!

We went on searching for the perfect match. The first foster house we went to had a litter of lab puppies. Seeing eight new puppies playing in a pin that night was like I had just stepped onto the first cloud in heaven, just true bliss. I knew I would find her there.

Olive was the first dog that came and sat on my lap that evening. She immediately put her head on my chest and that was it. I was completely smitten. Olive had picked me out that day and I knew she would be the perfect match.

I was finally able to take her home a couple days after New Year's Day. She was immediately spoiled with love and toys. Everyone fell in love her instantly. As she grew, our connection grew stronger and it was known she was mine and I was hers.

I never thought about making her a service dog because I didn't need "service". It wasn't until a month or so after Route 91 that the thought even passed my mind. Talking with my therapist, we agreed that it would be a great idea to get her registered as my emotional support or service animal. When conducting my research, I noticed that PTSD falls under the "Service Dog" category. I thought that she would have been categorized as "Emotional Support" but I didn't mind what she was going to be labeled as, I just wanted to know that I could take her wherever I needed.

With having flashbacks on a regular basis and having that constant worry that something horrific might occur, I knew being able to take her with me would be the right choice. It wasn't until February 2018 that she officially became a Service Dog. I loved being able to take her with me and it gave me a sense of ease.

Having Olive around whenever and wherever was such a great feeling. She brought me more comfort than I imagined. Everywhere we went together people just wanted to pet her and adored her.

As I started taking her more places, I noticed people's reactions when they saw me with her and her "Service Dog" vest. People would look at her, then up at me, then back down at her with eyes of judgment. I could see the thoughts racing through their minds as if I had x-ray vision. "Why does she need a service dog", "She looks fine to me", "I bet she doesn't even need a service dog". People don't need to say anything; actions speak louder than words.

Not everyone gives such judgmental looks, but most do. The people who aren't being judgmental, either ask to pet her or just go right up and pet her without asking for permission. When strangers just randomly come up and start petting her it takes me aback. I remember growing up and seeing a service dog in public and just itching to go pet it. My mom always told me I couldn't pet it or distract the dog because it was working. The burning sensation of eagerness filled me up almost instantly when I was told I couldn't pet a cute fluffy dog that was within arms-reach.

To this day, I still get that urge but now, after experiencing having a dog that is providing me service and support, I completely understand the awkward feeling when people pet Olive when she has her vest on. I, of course, want to share her with the world because she is an incredible dog and extremely sensitive and sweet but at the same time, I never know when a flashback or panic attack will occur.

If someone is petting Olive and all of a sudden something happens, I need people to understand and not take offense when I kindly ask them to stop or I walk away. It's definitely a weird place to be in but I think just being open and honest to people helps.

There was one morning when Olive and I were running on the beach. It was early morning around 6:30 am, so not many people were out. For the most part, I keep Olive on leash but there are parts along the beach where she runs off leash and stays right by my side.

We were finishing up the last strip of beach, I had my headphones on, and I was trying to finish strong. This man that was headed in our direction and waves me down to get my attention.

We stop and I take off my headphones to listen to what he had to say.

"You're breaking the rules," said this stranger.

"Excuse me?" I responded.

"You can't have dogs on the beach," he begins to inspect her as if he were a judge in a dog show, "Oh, she is a service dog?" he asks.

"Yea, she is a service dog," I respond.

"Well are you good?" He asks questioning my appearance.

"Yeah…but I need her when I run."

I glance down and around to make sure I didn't miss something in our surroundings to figure out why I would not look okay.

"Well then why do you need a service dog?" He asks condescendingly.

"Because I have PTSD." I respond as politely as I could.

"PTSD? From what?" He asks doubtingly.

"From being shot at." I answer.

"Where? On the streets or something?" He asks.

"No, from the mass shooting in Las Vegas, last October at the Route 91concert. So, I need her when I run to prevent flashbacks." I respond with some detail thinking one of the key words would trigger something in his head.

"Never heard of it." He says.

"I said well it was one of the largest mass shootings. It happened October 1st, 2017 in Las Vegas at a country concert." I said firmly.

"Oh, well you're good though right?" He responds.

"Yea" I said briefly.

"Well stay good." He said.

"Have a great day." I said and took off running to the end of the beach.

I charged up the hill to the top where my car was parked. I was fuming after that conversation. I couldn't believe the ignorance and the tone he had with his interrogation.

That moment really got me thinking on how people perceive someone with a service dog when there isn't any physical scaring or handicap. People don't realize the toll a mental scar or mental illness can have on a person. Someone may look completely fine on the outside but when you begin to open up this perfectly wrapped casing you begin to see the broken pieces and bruises and dents inside someone.

You really can't judge a book by its cover because we all have inner issues, demons, cuts, scars, mysteries behind our shinning smiles and well-kept clothes.

After leaving the beach that day, I cried the whole way home. On that 15-minute drive, I saw a car with a "Route 91" sticker. Seeing that sticker helped bring me out of the fiery red tunnel I was engrossed in. It brought the light at the end of the passageway. It helped me realize that there are going to people out there that don't understand. I needed to push past that and know that there are 22,000 people and counting who will understand and be there for me.

A similar situation happened about a year after that run in. It was on the same beach, with a similar looking man. Once again, it was early morning, so not many people on the beach.

We were finishing up our run and we were walking toward the ramp to go up to my car. This man literally came up from the shoreline to talk with me.

He said the same thing as the first guy, "You're breaking the rules".

I responded, "No, she is a service dog".

Now his response, instantly turned the clear blue morning into bright red. I was suddenly heated and angry at this man's ignorance.

He said, "Service dogs and emotional support animals aren't real."

I swear to you it took every ounce of energy not to knock this guy on his butt. I was shocked in his response.

I responded, "Excuse me? Yes, they do." pointing down at Olive.

He responded in a snarky attitude, "You don't look blind. You don't need a service dog."

I felt pools filling in my eyes as I held back all the words I so desperately wanted to scream at this man. What if I had been in the military or had epilepsy? Then this guy would have felt like a real ass.

I responded as calmly as I could, "I have PTSD and PTSD falls under the category of service animal, go home and do your research".

He walked away waving us down and I angrily started my journey up the steps to my car. I immediately texted my boyfriend Alex venting to him what had just happened and then called my mom. I sobbed to my mom on the phone all the way up the dreaded hill. It was embarrassing climbing the hill in tears calling my mom like I'm a 5-year-old on the playground telling my mom that boy over there called me stupid. But I felt more embarrassed for the man on the beach.

I felt embarrassed that he lives a life where he feels the need to put people down. He literally has nothing else going on besides telling people what he thinks is right or wrong instead of listening and learning. I felt embarrassed for his family, that they have to be surrounded by his negativity and ignorance.

The man on the beach that specific morning tore down a wall I had built since the first guy. He broke me but only for a minute. I wasn't going to give him the win over a battle I've been fighting for over a year.

I couldn't let one ass hole bring me down and neither should you or anyone else. Don't let someone's ignorance domineer your progress and success. I was finally back to running and doing something I love. I wouldn't let one person stand in my way.

Running was a huge obstacle for me for months after Route 91. I have always been into fitness and working out. I didn't "enjoy" running until high school when I realized I was lapping the boys on my second mile when they were on their first.

I was terrified to run after Route 91 because I had just ran for my life. Running along streets or buildings was an absolute no so I tried running the beach. It definitely was a step in the right direction, but I still had my moments.

Running with Olive on the beach was the perfect cure to my new fear of running. Whenever I would feel like my memory was pulling me back into darkness of that night, I would just look down at her happy puppy face looking back at me. It was like magic. The cure to this sickness and disease.

I not only took Olive with me on our beach runs, but I started taking her to more places, like the grocery store and restaurants. The judgmental looks followed, especially at restaurants.

The only place I never received these looks of hostility was at the airport. The February after Route 91, my mom and grandmother (with whom I lived with) moved to Washington to live with my uncle. So, when Olive became my service dog that month, it was perfect timing because now, I could fly with her.

The first time we flew together was April 2018 when we went up to Washington for Easter. Having Olive there with me made the journey up there so much more relaxing. It's incredible how dogs can relieve so much stress from daily situations. Especially a dog you have a strong relationship with.

When I planned on returning to Washington for Thanksgiving, I needed to stay with my cousin Daniel the night before since I was flying out of LAX at 6am and he lives in LA. My aunt and my other cousin Darin decided to take me up the day before and we made a day out of it.

While we were out window-shopping and enjoying holiday lights, I noticed how surrounded we were, by people and buildings. The area we were walking around was absolutely packed. At times, it made me uncomfortable and I was constantly watching the tops of buildings and people's reactions. I felt safe for the most part but with having to travel so early in the morning the next day and being surrounded by so much was very overwhelming.

We were standing by a gigantic Christmas tree when little kids came up and started petting Olive. With them being such small children, I tried to not let it bother me that they didn't ask or even acknowledge my presence, but it was the parent's reactions that truly impacted me.

The parents didn't even try to teach them that you can't walk up to any dog and pet them. They just started petting Olive and kept following us as we would take steps in other directions.

This interaction with people that were so oblivious to the fact that you shouldn't touch a service dog was shocking to me. It really helped change my way of thinking about others that have service dogs that assist with serious medical conditions like epilepsy.

So, with my encounters with individuals that are disrespectful, oblivious, or sending negative thoughts my way, this is my message to you. Please don't interact with dogs if you think they may be a service dog or if they have a sign saying "Service" or "Emotional Support". Just because a person may "seem fine" doesn't mean they are fine. It's better to not interact and cause a disruption to the dog and the owner because you never know what they may be going through internally.

Imagine if you walked up to a service dog and started petting it and taking pictures or distracting it from its job to protect its owner and that person ended up having a seizure. Where that dog was supposed to give warning and alert the owner and those around of what is about to take place. If that were me, I would feel absolutely terrible.

So do your best to imagine what the worst possible outcome could be if you go up to a service dog without asking first. I don't want anyone to feel uncomfortable or be caused pain because of something that could have easily been avoided. Respect the owner's words and actions and don't overstay your welcome. If the owner says, "that's enough" or gives you any indication that it's time to stop, be respectful and stop. I never want to make someone feel bad for wanting to pet and play with Olive but if the time comes when I need her, I don't want strangers lingering around like party guests that over stayed their welcome.

So, stop, think, ask, respect.

Chapter 9
Thoughts, Feelings, & More

This chapter is filled with all the extra details about life with PSTD. From dating and relationships, to music, to work, and anything and everything else that didn't fit into its own chapter. I've broken it apart into sections for an easier read.

Dating

Dating after living through such a traumatic event is challenging. Just living your life is hard enough, then throw dating in the mix and it's the perfect combination of chaos. Part of you wants someone there to comfort and love and the other part of you just wants to be alone and believes you will be alone forever. Who could love someone who is so broken and how long will this brokenness last?

I was in a relationship when Route 91 happened. I thought this maybe could be "the one" but I only thought that after I almost died. I think the only reason we lasted as long as we did was because of Route 91. Maybe he felt bad and didn't want to break up with a girl who was emotionally unstable. Everyone wanted us to work but we obviously didn't, and I knew deep down we wouldn't work out together. I wasn't getting what I wanted from the relationship and you shouldn't have to settle.

We were pretty solid until October 1, 2017. The moment I realized that I might die that night, I thought I loved Austen. I wanted so badly to say, "I love you" to him and my mom. That's all that raced through my mind. But in the moment of destruction and despair your mind reaches the furthest corners of your mind and aches for your longest hopes and desires, whether they are what you really want or think you want. I didn't tell him I loved him that night. I actually never told him. But in the moment, I wanted to tell him, but I knew if I did, I would die. That's how every story ends. You send that last text, or you whisper your last breath saying the words that you desperately want to say to someone just so you feel that you ended life on the high of love.

Well we made it to just over 6 months after Route 91. We broke up right after we reached our one-year mark. I had thoughts about ending it earlier but thought it was just "cold feet" or my PTSD getting the best of me. But he ended it on a Tuesday night, as I was cooking him dinner.

He was in school full time after quitting his job to be a firefighter paramedic. I felt worthless and cooking him dinner and trying to make his life easier gave me purpose. That night when he ended it, it crushed me, but only for a few days. Deep down inside, I knew it was the right decision. I knew we weren't supposed to be together, but it still hurt. I had put so much effort into the relationship for a whole year and for such a crucial 6 months of my life. Part of me is glad he was there and another part of me wishes he wasn't there.

When I had gotten home from Vegas that Monday, I had seen my mother and grandmother before anyone else. Austen was the first person outside of my family I saw. I wanted that moment to be just like the movies, filled with passion and an embracing hug and kiss but it wasn't. I should have known then that we were destined for doom from the moment I saw him after Vegas. It seemed so dull. It wasn't anything like I expected. I honestly was disappointed.

I had envisioned our reaction over and over again in my head on that four- and half-hour car ride home. Just as I had imagined how my interaction with my mom would be. But both felt numb. I felt more disappointed in the interaction with Austen though. I consider myself a hopeless romantic, hopeless being the main adjective. I expected hugs, passionate kisses, words of endearment but I got just our typical interaction. A hug, a kiss, and a "how are you". My faith diminished slightly with that encounter with the guy I thought I loved just 9 hours prior.

After Austen and I broke up, dating was hard. I was on dating apps and would go on dates, but it was weird. When does one bring up that they almost died less than 1 year ago?

I had gone out on multiple dates and it seemed to come up in almost every first date, like word vomit it spilled out on the table we shared. I didn't want to scare my dates off, but this was a part of my life now and if someone couldn't handle on it on a first date, how could they in the future?

It seemed like the only guys I could even have a relationship with from now on, had to be country fans because they were the only ones that would understand. It was usually because they had friends that went to Route 91, they almost went themselves, or because they're engrossed in the country music community, like me, where we share this bond.

I had casually dated a few different guys, but nothing seemed like the right fit. I even occasionally dipped in the friends with benefits thing thinking that would help fill my needs since I couldn't fill the shoes of the "perfect girlfriend" (sorry mom).

In the end nothing truly felt like it would work, at least not long term. When you're single, living with PSTD, it feels like you will never find someone who can "put up with it".

They say you live with PSTD forever, so how would I ever be in a serious relationship again? It seemed like when the "right" guy would come around, I would find a reason to shut them down and not go with it. I was scared of anyone seeing my nightmares, my anxiety, or a flashback. I couldn't dare put that on someone. My friends and family had seen enough of it, I didn't want to bring someone else into these problems, it wasn't fair to them or me.

I know that one day, someone will come into my life that's supposed to be there and will stay and will be there for me through the good and the bad days. But in the end, I have to make sure I open myself up to it and allow people to come in and give them a chance to understand.

Unfortunately, I have to be able to accept lots of rejection from people and I know that will hurt but that's how it's going to be from now on until Mr. Right finds his way into my life. It's so unfortunate but this is the reality of something traumatic happening in your life. People are not as strong as you and can't deal with being with someone that isn't "100% there".

People don't want to date someone that's "damaged goods" but in reality, we all are whether we like it or not and don't want to admit to it. We either have a troubled past, have PTSD, have been cheated on and have trust issues, maybe don't even know who we truly are, struggle with commitment issues or addiction, struggle with mounds of debt, or just aren't a very good person.

But before you include someone in your own problems and issues, make sure you're at least happy with yourself and the decisions you make on a daily basis. It's hard to come back from something traumatic, like a mass shooting, you are a completely different person after that, but you will eventually learn to love yourself again. Just hang in there and someone will love you, the new you.

I'll tell you one thing is for sure. If you're trying to date after living through an event similar to Route 91, just be open and honest. Don't be afraid to show who you are now. If that person can't handle it or doesn't want to be a part of it, just leave and move on. You've already been through enough you don't need more negativity and hurt in your life.

Your right person will take you as you are, bumps, bruises, hurts, and hang ups. They will take you as you are because they will see you differently than you see yourself. It may take months or even years but just be patient and focus on yourself and your happiness first.

People are drawn to happiness, laughter, fun, and love. If you aren't focusing on the things that make you happy, that make you laugh, the fun times, and things you love, you aren't showing the best sides of you. So, don't stress on how terrible the date went because you had a flashback, don't worry about the ass hole that didn't text you after the first date because you told him you have PTSD. Your person is out there but make sure you're happy with yourself first before you can be happy with them.

Work

Work is a whole other subject. Like I said in previous chapters, working in a classroom setting was challenging. With the amount of school shootings occurring monthly, if not weekly, I was terrified to be the classroom setting again. There was no way in hell I could live through two shootings in my life. Living through one was hard enough.

This first year was hard and no one wanted to take a chance on a teacher who has PTSD. I went through a handful of interviews and in every interview the question came up on "is there anything that could prevent you from holding out your duties as a teacher" or "what are your weaknesses" or something along those lines. As an honest person, I thought that it would only be right and fair to address my PTSD head on. Of course, that failed me on nearly every interview.

The second they heard that, I saw the brick and mortar walls build and I was instantly shut out and denied without given a chance. The only school that took a chance on me was HCA and honestly it was where I needed to be and where I was happy. I realized that all those schools that rejected me after the first or second interview were not the schools I needed to be at.

When I came back from Las Vegas and I was offered a teaching position to teach Kindergarten in Yorba Linda and I tried so hard to make it work. But if something is the right fit, it shouldn't require *that* much of an effort, it should flow easily, for the most part. Work will still be work but you should at least enjoy it.

When I had the moment of a flashback in the classroom, I thought I would never be able to teach in the classroom again. I saw my whole college career flush down the toilet, all the hard work, late nights, and money funnel down the water tube into the rat filled drains that lead to the ocean. I hated that but at the same time thought maybe there is a reason behind this.

I only stayed at the school in Yorba Linda for a few weeks before having to resign. I knew I couldn't put this on my resume and felt like I had wasted their time and mine. I felt like I failed at the one thing I was trained to do for a living. I saw everything crash before me and I cried but accepted it.

Thankfully I was offered a position to work with a 4th grade student who has autism at an office a few hours a day, five days a week. It seemed like a great job for a while, the pay was great, the hours were great, but I still felt the need to teach in the classroom setting. I felt like I wasn't reaching my potential but at the same time knew I wasn't ready. I needed to take care of my well-being.

It took the whole school year of working with private home-schooled clients for me to be completely ready to apply for full time classroom teaching jobs again. I went on more interviews than I could count. But of course, fear was in their eyes when PTSD was mentioned because I had a "gap" year of teaching in a classroom setting.

I got asked, "Are you sure you're ready" in almost every interview. I thought I wasn't going to be able to teach again because I didn't want to lie to people. HCA opened their doors and hearts to me.

It was the perfect set up because it was a part time position teaching 3rd grade two days a week and then I could work with my private clients the other three days. It was the bridge I needed from unemployment to teaching. I knew with only being in the classroom setting two days a week, I could still focus on my healing, but I still got to teach to a class. I wouldn't be jumping into the deep end of teaching in the classroom 5 days a week with trying to focus on recovering.

As I am completing this book, I am diving into my second year there and about to teach 8th grade. I know, what am I thinking teaching middle school students. But in all honesty, I feel like it's where I was destined to be, I can now use everything I have learned to really help these kids.

Maybe one day, I will go back into teaching 5 days a week, but I realize now, that whatever is meant to be will be, I can't stress about it. If I didn't take this chance and if they didn't take this chance on me, I wouldn't be where I am today.

If you're an employer and someone comes to you in an interview and has the faith and trust to admit something personal to you, try and see it as they don't want to lie to a potential employer. Someone is bearing their flesh and bones and still proving their potential to you in a 15-minute interview that they have been preparing for for days. Listen and have an open mind and heart. Just because someone has PTSD, or some baggage doesn't mean that they can't prove their worth professionally.

If you're a survivor struggling to keep a job or find a job, don't worry it will take time for the right job to come around. It may not be what you envisioned or hoped for, but you will realize it's the right fit for where you're at in your life.

All the Extra Stuff

One thing that truly daunted on me was attending concerts. Now this will probably be different per person because we all suffer through a different kind of situation during our traumatic event. For me and all of our Route 91 family, concerts seemed impossible because the last one we had attended we almost died.

I went to my first concert on March 29th, 2018, nearly 6 months after Route 91. It wasn't a country concert, it was indoors, and I had been to this venue before, which I think was a smart idea for me for my first concert after the Route 91 concert. I had gone with my boyfriend at the time and he was very understanding of everything that night.

I made sure we didn't go into the middle and we stayed near the back, with no one behind us, and I kept a close look out. I was constantly watching all the exits and monitoring every person to make sure they weren't doing anything suspicious. I made it through the whole concert and was so excited I did it. On our way to the car, I started to get anxious because a handful of us concert goers were walking back to our cars like a slow marching stampede, in between

136

office buildings. Having that many people walking together in such a confined area, made me nervous.

After successfully surviving that concert, I decided to push myself a little more. A month later, I went to a country bar. I had missed line dancing and being surrounded by liked minded people. I went with my friend Victoria who is also a Route 91 survivor.

It was challenging and I had my moments, but I was so proud of myself for going out of my comfort zone and trying it again. It soon became a weekly ritual that we would go line dancing every Thursday. Every week was different. Some weeks we're flawless, other weeks I was running out of the bar in tears due to a flashback or anxiety.

The thing I want you to take from this is that, it's going to be hard, you're going to freak out, have anxiety, or bail halfway through but you have to put yourself back out there when the time feels right. Take little steps to get yourself back to the things you loved before your life changed. It took me over 6 months to step foot in a country bar again, but I go, and I continue to go no matter what. It's okay to take your time and hold back from certain things but at least try. If you fail and realize you can't do that thing again, at least you gave it a chance.

Another thing I took a chance on was running. Running was definitely hard for a while because I had just ran for my life. So, when I would run, it gave me severe anxiety and triggered flashbacks. After I started making some progress in my healing, I wanted to push myself with running. I decided to complete a 10k race. I had been running on the beach with Olive, but I wanted a goal to achieve, a purpose for our running.

I knew I couldn't do it without her, so we ran our first 10k race together on Memorial Day 2018. I had her by my side the whole race and I was so impressed we did it. We ended up doing another in November of that year. Once I started looking at running as achieving a goal of beating my personal record or completing a race, I stopped looking at it as I was overcoming my PTSD and flashbacks.

I think giving running more of a purpose outside of accomplishing goals mentally. It helped me get back into the groove of it and enjoy it again. Now I don't really think about the "what ifs" with running and it rarely triggers any anxiety of flashbacks. I've proven to myself that I can do it with or without Olive and still succeed. Since then, I have accomplished something I never dreamed I would do. I completed a half marathon and will hopefully do another one in the future.

Lastly, if you are a survivor of a shooting, you'll understand how holidays, crowded events, or certain occasions trigger anxiety and flashbacks. I know most of us from Route 91 dread the 4th of July. Hearing fireworks from all different directions can be extremely alarming and the sound is so similar to that of a gun. We all believed, when the shooting started, that it was just fireworks until we actually saw the destruction.

I know for me personally and a handful of survivors I've talked with, any event or holiday that we know will have fireworks, triggers anxiety, fear, and flashbacks.

Leading up to holidays like 4th of July and New Year's Eve, I've had massive anxiety and panic attacks the whole week prior. My mind just racing around a racetrack; each bend a different "what if" or uncertainty of how I will respond. My mind just continues to race around, again and again, each lap triggering an anxiety attack or a flashback to that night. Until the actual event, then my heart just races, my senses on high alert, until the climax of it all, then comes the fall of utter exhaustion from my body being on full drive this whole time.

Almost every time, since Route 91, that I've heard fireworks, they have triggered flashbacks, sometimes more severe than others. It usually leads to me feeling depressed, defeated, and haunted. Depressed because fireworks used to be one of my favorite things in the world, I just loved the pure magic of not knowing what firework would come next and seeing such beauty in the dark of night. Defeated because no matter how many times I expose myself to them, it seems like it never gets easier. Haunted because I see everything so clearly, just as if I had time traveled back to that night.

People say this probably won't last forever or it will lessen over time and I sure hope they're right. Having something as simple as fireworks taken from you sucks and it ruins special occasions.

My goal or wish for people who don't understand this is to just be there for that person. Don't get mad or disappointed if this person doesn't want to go outside knowing fireworks will occur. Just be there and listen and know it's hard, it's extremely hard and they want to try or are trying.

Finally, I would like to leave with pieces of advice:

1. Don't worry about other people just focus on yourself during your time of healing. If someone isn't there to support you during this, they don't deserve you.
2. Know that everyone heals differently and at different times. The three of us all healed differently, even though we were there together. It's definitely hard to process that the person that was standing next to you

is perfectly fine, when you feel like your life is crumbling minute by minute.

3. Try. Try to get back to normal the best you can, at your own pace. As much as you want to be back to normal within a month or even a year, that might not be the case. People won't understand why you're still having flashbacks a year and half later and honestly you won't either. Healing from this might take a lifetime and you just need to understand and accept that.

4. Know that this happened to you for a reason. You may not see it right away, but you will realize it one day. You will see the good rising from the bad as long as you push through. Hang in there!

5. Find a way to get your ugly thoughts out of your head. Don't box them up and think everything will be okay if they're not addressed and brought to the surface. Express how you're really feeling even if you don't feel comfortable talking about it. What helped me was writing it all out. Maybe your way of expressing is kickboxing, painting, music, or talking with friends or a therapist. Just make sure you get those dark and disturbing thoughts out of your head so that you don't let them consume your mind.

6. Don't think that there is a time limit on when you need to be "back to normal". If you start putting that pressure on yourself, you'll never move forward. Focus on your accomplishments, big or small, each accomplishment is a step in the right direction.

7. It's okay to be scared. It's okay to feel depressed. It's okay to have anxiety. It's okay to feel completely and utterly in despair. Humans are wired to feel every emotion possible. What's not okay is to have these emotions control your life and your happiness. Find things that make you happy and try to change your thinking habits. That's what I did with the 6 Months of Happiness challenge, it helped change my thinking.

8. Know you're stronger than you believe. I have accomplished things I never thought I would accomplish because of Route 91. I can see my strength and feel the pride in all the hurdles and goals I've completed.

9. You may be good for a few days, weeks, or months and think you've beat it and then something will happen, and you will crumble and break again. Don't let that set you back. Look at how far you've come. If life didn't present us with problems and issues, it would be boring.

10. Know your true friends and family will stand by your side and know you might lose relationships. That is bound to happen because people panic in the face of change. The people who stand by your side, are who you want to keep around.

11. Lastly, know you're loved. Even by people you don't know. There are people out there that have also survived a tragic event just like you and they are thinking about you and wishing you the best. If you survive a mass shooting or a traumatic event, you're now a part of a club that has far too many members, but it's filled with love and support.

12. **You're not alone.**

Chapter 10

October 1, 2018

Leading up to the one-year anniversary of Route 91 has been so daunting. I personally don't know what to feel and when to feel it. I decided to start this chapter on August 1, 2018. It's been 10 months since the night that changed my life forever and so much has happened, so much has changed. For months and months after, it felt like October 1, 2018 was light-years away. I never thought I would make it to this point and where I am in my life. I am starting this chapter on a Wednesday night looking out at the sunset at the beach and thinking back on these past 10 months. I never really gave much thought to the one-year anniversary until recently.

Today has been challenging thinking that it marks 10 months and that there are only 2 months left. Just a couple weeks ago I decided to go back to Las Vegas for the one-year anniversary. Until then, it seemed like October 1, 2018 would never happen. It was a distant thought that felt like a mirage, like it wasn't and wouldn't be real. I talked to my friends and therapist a lot about it and I thought back to how over a year ago, in the beginning of 2017, I said I wasn't going to let anything stop me, how I was going to accomplish my dreams and goals. Well if I don't go back to

Las Vegas for the reunion I am letting fear stop me. I am letting fear take over. I know it's going to be very emotional and difficult, but I feel like when I go it will close another chapter in my life.

When I made the decision a couple weeks to go back to Las Vegas I talked with my therapist about it before talking to anyone else. She is the one that knows everything; she is the one I trust with *almost* all my secrets from the past 10 months (some things I haven't told anyone). After getting her thoughts and advice I called my mom immediately after my session with Cindy asking if she would meet me in Vegas for the reunion. I was nervous calling her because I know how crazy her work schedule is and how tough it would be for her to fly down from Washington. She told me she would do what she could to come down and be there for me.

My roommate/friend Becca said she would go with me as well and it felt great to know I have a friend and my mom attending with me on this weekend. I had asked several friends and family members if they would join and they all had different excuses and reasons why they couldn't attend. Honestly, it felt heartbreaking hearing some of my closest friends not even attempt to make an effort, just saying they can't because of "work".

After living through something like this, you truly realize who your true friends are and who are just friends. It makes you start to notice a person's character traits more because your senses, feelings, and emotions are heightened.

I've known Becca and her family for 10 years, but we never really connected or became good friends until we moved in together in February 2018 with another one of my friends. Since moving in together, she has been one of my biggest support systems. Becca has been there for all the good and bad days.

August 28th, 32 days until Las Vegas, was one of those difficult days.

Every day Facebook gives you a reminder of all the things you posted about on that day since you've had Facebook. Sometimes it's awesome because you look back and see happy memories, other days it's depressing. Today wasn't one of those happy memory days. It was a "flashback" into the past of the day our Route 91 bracelets arrived in the mail.

I remember getting that package in the mail and getting so excited. I had already picked out majority of my outfits and just wanted to put the bracelet on that day. Seeing that post from 1 year ago crushed my heart and soul for what seemed like the millionth time in the past 11 months. I was already having a challenging week with this being the last week of summer before I go back to teaching the next week and knowing that Saturday marked 11 months since that horrific night. Then being reminded of something that once made me smile but now haunted me wasn't the greatest addition to my week.

All day that bracelet raced through my mind and the blood that stained the purple fabric. I wanted so badly to keep that bracelet and make something beautiful from it in remembrance, but I had to cut off the second I got home on October 2nd, 2017. I couldn't stand to see the blood of the person next to me any longer. I wanted it gone and now here it is again, back on my phone screen, haunting me.

I had shared that memory with the caption, "Well this sucks". I wasn't expecting to get a huge response, but I was shocked with how certain comments made me feel. People said things such as, "Block those posts", "But look how far you've come", and "stay strong" and surprisingly, it only made me mad. I couldn't believe after all this time people continued to not know what to say or how to say it or maybe I was just being over sensitive. Either way, those words hurt and made me welt up with anger. Only one comment made me feel somewhat at peace and it stated, "Praying for you and all of Route 91". Seeing that comment was exactly what "I" (without knowing it) needed and wanted to hear. I didn't need to hear people's thoughts and opinions on what they think I should do, but just be there and say supportive words. I've heard people tell me what I should do for the past 11 months and it only makes me angrier and angrier because they didn't know or understand.

Fast forward to Friday September 28th, 2018, the day we left for Vegas. Becca, her mom Tammy, and I flew together, with Becca and I sitting next to each other. Becca asked to read the first chapter of my book so she could get a better understanding of what happened that night. I felt incredibly nervous having her read my story while I sat inches away. It didn't help I was already feeling every emotion possible knowing where I was going and why I was going there.

We landed in Vegas around 4:00 p.m. and I instantly wanted to look for anything to distract me from feeling my emotions. I wanted so desperately to become numb, I wanted to flash through this weekend and have it be over. Most importantly I didn't want to see the site, I didn't want to see the hotel. I was scared of what may come over me.

After leaving the airport and driving past Mandalay Bay for the first time, I just flipped it off. I was overcome with anger. I imagined it exploding and crumbling to the ground and disappearing from all existence. I knew it was going to be a looming tower of hatred and pain all weekend and I knew it wasn't going to disappear, as much as I wanted, so I just needed to do my best to ignore it.

Becca, her mom, and I decided to head off to dinner on the strip. I was nervous about being on the strip again and I was in constant alert of what was going on around us the whole time. But I had made it through dinner and was actually able to eat some of my food, and my nerves didn't quite take over my whole stomach.

Later that night, my cousin Daniel arrived in town. He came to support me, even though he was only going to be there for less than 24 hours. Having him there almost put a shield of safety and protection over my fears and anxiety. Him and I have always been close and so it was such an incredible feeling having him there, especially since my mom wasn't arriving until the next day.

It was a weird feeling that night. I didn't want to go to sleep; I didn't want to close my eyes while being in Vegas. I was nervous as to what might happen if I do. What if something tragic happens? What if I have nightmares? My mind was scrambling around looking for distraction and answers.

The next morning, we woke up early to go volunteer at the healing garden. We spent the morning planting flowers and cleaning up our memorial garden. It was challenging because the spot we picked to start, was the area dedicated to our angel Kelsey.

It shook me seeing the name Kelsey and thinking, that could have been me. I completely lost it and that night started flooding back instantly. I felt isolated again, even though I was surrounded by fellow survivors and family. I didn't want to show what I was feeling. I didn't want to be asked if I was okay, I just wanted to be alone because I already felt alone.

I was able to calm myself and control my emotions even though some tears were shed. We toured the garden and I came across my mom's friend's area for Tommy Day. I made sure to take pictures and help in his area because I wasn't sure I would have the strength to come back.

After our time at the garden, we went back to the hotel to shower and freshen up. I took as long as I could in the shower. I needed time to process everything. In that shower, it felt as though I kept trying wash off my feelings, but I could never completely wash away the internal dirt my soul was blanketed with. I wanted so desperately to come out of the shower feeling fresh and clean, but I didn't.

After, we decided to do a complete 180 from the sorrowful morning we had, and we went to a drag brunch. It was just the type of distraction and entertainment I needed but I didn't feel like I was completely there. It was almost as if my soul was outside of my body, watching and begging for me to feel whole again. Not even the mounds of food on my plate or the buckets of mimosas could make me feel full.

After our eventful brunch, we made our way back to our hotel to wait for my mom to arrive. I was anxious to see my mom. I hadn't seen her since the beginning of April, for Easter. I was nervous to have her see me in such a vulnerable state. No one wants to admit they're hurting or need assistance; everyone wants to prove they are brave and strong, especially around loved ones.

I was thrilled she was making the trip down to be here to support me, but I didn't want her to see the dark, the ugly, the things that scared me most. She is my mother and her job is to protect me but this time she couldn't protect me, she couldn't stop the pain, the hurt, and she couldn't remove the thoughts that haunted my brain. I didn't want her to feel helpless, I didn't want her to feel frustrated or defeated that she couldn't fully be there for me no matter how much she tried.

Seeing her did help, it almost made the weekend feel less horrifically terrifying. I still felt the heavy weighted blanket of guilt and anxiety, but it was like it was slightly lifted. Like when you're hot in the middle of the night but you don't want to get cold, so you just let your foot hang out of the blanket a little, so you get that light breeze, that's what it felt like. I still felt the weight, but I had a light breeze cooling off some of those inner demons.

That evening the five of us went to Top Golf. We enjoyed appetizers, beers, and the freedom to hit golf balls as far as we wanted. It started off as a stress-free evening. The weather was perfect, the beer was chilled just right, and funny stories and laughs were shared around the table.

When I realized our time was running out, a dark cloud of realism gloomed over my head. I came to the conclusion that my cousin would be leaving when we finished up and that I would have to go back to the reality that the reunion was still approaching.

It was a nice escape while it lasted but like all good things, it had to come to an end. Walking out of Top Golf, everything hit like a tidal wave. We were surrounded by buildings and the sound of helicopters overhead, sent me running to hide. I went into flashback mode and went behind the building away from streets and open access. I stood there shaking, paranoid, searching for answers or anything that could get me stop. I wanted everything to freeze. I needed time to examine my situation, I needed help but felt like I couldn't ask for it. It was almost as if the words were stripped from my vocabulary. I couldn't murmur those words; they were stolen from me.

My mom came to comfort me. She helped talk me out of the flashback. She helped bring me to reality. If she wasn't there to help bring me back, I was afraid I never would. It took what seemed like years for me to come back to reality in that moment. I struggled coming to reality because I knew my cousin was leaving and we were in Vegas, surrounded by the same sounds and the same buildings that were there nearly a year ago.

After coming back from my extended stay in flashback central, I had to say goodbye to my cousin. It was the hardest goodbye I had ever had with him. I didn't want him to leave. Him leaving, meant that I had to keep moving forward with the weekend. It meant that I had one less shelter of protection. Seeing him leave hurt, it hurt more than I thought it would, but I was incredibly thankful he came. Words couldn't even describe how thankful I was and still am that he came all that way for one night.

After he left, we started gearing up for the night. We had tickets to go to Gilly's at Treasure Island for a Route 91 evening. I was excited because I knew I was going to be surrounded by my Route 91 family but nervous because we were all back together again, country dancing in Las Vegas, and the last time this happened, we were shot at.

Subconsciously, I knew that a similar situation would be extremely rare, but it was still a thought rummaging around in the back of my mind.

I had ran into some friends from Cowboy Country back home in Long Beach and that helped ease tension because it started to feel like home and feel familiar. I had the courage to ask the DJ if he could make an announcement for all Route 91 family to take a group picture and it worked.

We got an incredible group photo to remember the strength we were facing that night. I look back at that photo from time to time and even though I don't know everyone, it still feels like a family photo.

The next day, Sunday September 30th, 2018, was filled with football and junk food. I didn't want to think about the day that was coming. I just wanted things to feel normal. I distracted myself with beer, wings, and football games. We had a great day the four of us, hoping from bar to bar watching games and just relaxing.

Even though most of the day went okay, I still had two anxiety attacks at brunch, during our first stop. Knowing and anticipating what was in store, scared the shit out of me. I had felt light headed and like I was having an out of body experience which was rare since I hadn't had one this bad for years.

I was able to get myself out of them and move forward but that fear did linger all day.

That night, we had tickets to a benefit concert at Stoney's. I was on edge the whole night. It was extremely packed, and that night just felt so strangely similar to a year ago since the shooting happened on a Sunday night, even though I knew it wasn't the actual reunion night. There was just something overpowering my logical thinking that made me think that at 10:02, something was going to happen.

As you're reading this, it's obvious that nothing did happen that night but after living through something that traumatic, you can't help but think that something bad will happened again, especially on the same weekend.

Since we purchased certain tickets, we got Vegas Strong t-shirts which surprisingly were refreshing to receive that night, I was thankful that we decided to pay a little extra to get the shirts. I realized at that moment; I would have regretted it if we didn't.

This night, just like the last, was filled with dancing and I saw my same friends. Becca and I got our moms to do the Wobble dance and it was a great time. I didn't want to stop dancing. I didn't want the clock to strike midnight. I didn't want that harsh reality to hit, knowing it was the actual date of the reunion. Everyone wanted to leave at a reasonable hour, but I didn't want to. I knew we would go

155

back to the hotel and that would be it, the next day would come. I kept thinking if we just keep dancing and drinking, it won't happen. I won't have to deal with the truth. But I had to.

In the cab ride to our hotel, the clock hit midnight and I saw the date, October 1st, 2018. It hit me harder than I ever imagined. Seeing that and realizing what was in store for me as the day progressed was something I could never put into words. It's something every survivor and warrior must go through and no matter what I say or what anyone says, it won't make it easier. You just have to push through it and gain your badge of courage for toughing out an extremely challenging day.

After returning to our hotel that early morning, we went to sleep to try and obtain the maximum amount of sleep we could since we had an early start for the reunion. It was hard to sleep that night, but I was able to get in a couple hours.

We had to wake up extra early to arrive at the reunion ceremony. It was planned to start around 6:30/7:00 am and I didn't want to miss a thing. I wanted to take it all in and remember those that lost their life.

Within minutes of arriving, I was asked to be interviewed by Fox 11 news on my experience. I was already nervous and shaking being there, and I am not a fan of public speaking or being on television because I get incredibly nervous. You might not be able to tell but I get severe anxiety about it.

The newscaster had asked me about that night, what I experienced, and how I am coping with everything now. I told her and the everyone watching about the man that shot next to me, how the 6 Months of Happiness challenge helped me, and to always tell the people you love that you love them.

After my interview I joined back up with my mom, Becca, and her mom. We stood there crying and watching the ceremony unfold in front of our weary eyes. They had speakers, they honored first responders, and they had music. They released 58 doves that seemed to circle our area for quite some time. We all stood there in awe with tears streaming down our faces.

It was seemed that our voices were stripped away from us for minutes at a time while our brains were trying to process everything around us in that moment.

The ceremony lasted an hour, but it seemed to last a lifetime. I didn't want it to end but at the same time I wanted the day to be over. I didn't want to feel this heavy weight on my body anymore, I wanted to be set free like the doves. When it did end, we noticed a therapy dog behind us, and I held the dog as much as I could. He was the biggest dog I had seen in a long time and he was so loving. It the exact sign of love and support we needed in that moment.

Then came another interview.

It struck me as odd that I kept getting picked to be questioned and interviewed but I knew I was going to write a book and share my story anyways, so why not start now, I guess. Luckily this was a pen and paper interview and I didn't have to worry about appearing on television. Similar questions were asked, and similar answers were given.

After this interview we decided to head inside the building near the ceremony where crosses and memorials were placed for a viewing and honoring of that night. I had seen the crosses back in November and they were filled with treasures and tokens of love. Now, they were bare and stood as soldiers all lined up in perfect formation.

They had giant walls where you could write messages and prayers. They even had a case of wired angels and were handing these angels out as tokens on love and support.

It was an eerie feeling being in there, but it also felt like it was needed in my healing process. I needed to process everything and take moments to pray and heal.

We left the area and once again I felt like I had left a part of soul behind. This time it didn't feel as haunting as the morning we left Las Vegas one-year prior, but I still felt slightly lighter than when we arrived.

Our next stop was the Healing Garden. We walked around, took time to say little prayers for every person, and of course I was interviewed again. She took photos and asked some questions.

There was also a wedding that took place there, which made me uncomfortable. I understood their reasoning behind it, but I still couldn't shake the feeling of utter disrespect that couple had. I wanted to be happy for them because they survived together, made it through a year of PTSD together, and here they were reclaiming their freedom from PTSD and that night. I just couldn't see past it though and that hurt.

It hurt because I am all for a romantic story but this time, I didn't want it. It made me feel discombobulated and that sucked.

We left and headed to something that would lift our spirits and bring some lightheartedness to our day. We made our way to The Sugar Factory for lunch and drank fish bowls of sugar and alcohol. I had always wanted to come here, and I expected it to change my mood around, but it only shifted it slightly.

I went from being in a numb and depressed mood to feeling bitter sweet. I was happy to be there and to have survived the morning but at the same time I knew there was still half a day left to climb. I knew I was going to have to say goodbye to my mom and still make it to an event at the country bar I go to regularly. I was dreading how I would feel with these two "major" events left to occur that day.

Saying goodbye to my mom that day was one of the hardest goodbyes we've ever had. I was scared to be without her that evening. She had been there for me the past couple of days and I loved her being present. Now, I had to deal with the clock striking 10:02 without her.

After battling that battle of saying goodbye, we headed home. I knew once we arrived back home, I would have to freshen up and jump back in the car to head up to Long Beach. Cowboy Country is the place Jackie and I have gone to for months on a regular basis and they were holding an event for Route 91.

Fighting drowsiness, Becca made the 40-minute drive with me and I was so thankful she came with me. I expected to go alone because I couldn't imagine asking Becca for another favor after she just spent this whole weekend doing things and going to places for me.

Having her by my side that night helped immensely. We danced, laughed, and cried some more that night. Cowboy Country revealed a flag that they dedicated to Route 91 with a light that always shines on it, even to this day.

I was so proud to attend that night. I knew I couldn't have emotionally made it through the night in Vegas like some survivors did but to be surrounded by some of our family in a place that is special to me felt like I accomplished another obstacle in my path. It was challenging but I was glad I went, or I might have regretted not even trying.

I skipped work the next day. I felt bad calling for a sub, but I never want my students to see me in a funk, I always want to be the best version of myself for my students. I needed that day to sleep and recoup. The weekend was filled with so much emotion, stress, anxiety, and fear.

Going through the anniversary of Route 91 was hard, one of the hardest things to go through. Everyone that lives through a shooting will unfortunately have to go through it. It's a true struggle and test of your strength but surrounding yourself with people who love and care about you, helps massively.

If you're a survivor, it will be tough. I'm not going to sugar coat it. You might have flashbacks, anxiety, nightmares, and fear. As long as you stay positive and surround yourself with friends and family, you will be just fine. It's a process in your healing that you need to go through. You will come out stronger from it.

Friends and family just be there to listen, support, cry, and hug your friend or family member. We honestly can't process it all alone. We will need you there, whether it's letting us cry on your shoulder or just sitting in the same room as us. We are trying to process how a year ago our lives changed forever, and we almost died. It's a lot for our brains to process and we might not know exactly what we need.

If we fall silent, be silent with us. If we cry, hold us. If we get angry, give us grace.

Just be aware that just because the first year is over, doesn't mean it stops. You will start to have more good days than bad. You might still experience flashbacks and nightmares but over time it will lessen.

It will be hard to not be hard on yourself when you slip and have a moment. You may go months without having a flashback and then all of sudden they're back. It's a process that may last our lifetime but over time you will become stronger and fight through it all.

Just know you're stronger than you think and know you're loved and never alone. Do not fall victim to the thoughts that you're alone. People may heal quicker or differently but there are people that will listen and understand. Don't be afraid to reach out and ask for help when you need it. You're loved and you're strong.

Acknowledgments

Michelle M.

Beverly F.

Doreen F.

Daniel F.

Cindy F.

Becca M.

Tammy M.

Emily C.

Christopher A.

&

More...

Thank you to everyone that has helped me through this transition in my life. I am forever grateful for all that you have done to help support me.

Thank you for reading my story. I hope that it brought comfort, encouragement, or whatever you were hoping to gain out of it. My story is not over, and I will continue to share and help anyone and everyone I can.